ONLY FOR A FORTNIGHT

Only for a Fortnight

My life in a locked ward ▪ Sue Read

BLOOMSBURY

First published in Great Britain 1989
Reprinted January 1989
Second reprint February 1989

Copyright © 1989 by Sue Read
Bloomsbury Publishing Limited, 2 Soho Square, London W1V 5DE

ISBN 0–7475–0319–2

Typeset by Columns of Reading
Printed by Butler & Tanner Ltd, Frome and London

I dedicate my writings to Siobhan Helen.
She showed me that it truly is . . .
better to have loved and lost than never to have
loved at all.

ACKNOWLEDGEMENTS

To my husband, Steve, whose support, devotion and patience has made me whole.

To Sheryl, a much treasured daughter.

To Leslie, my long-time mentor and friend, who believed in me long before I believed in myself.

To my old mum, who's still here even after all we've been through together.

To my older sister, Pam, who visited me frequently, loaded with advice and small pressies.

To John Fairfax, who tutored me to make the most of my jumbled writings.

To Mr Fletcher, the Methodist Minister who gave unstinting support to my mum; also for his behind-the-scenes efforts to make the public aware of my dilemma.

To Helen, who became my firm friend during the harrowing time of my pregnancy and, later, Siobhan's death.

Finally, I acknowledge the FUTURE.

CONTENTS

NOTE

The author and publishers wish to point out that the names of some of the medical staff and other people referred to in this book have been altered to ensure their anonymity. Any similarity between any altered name and the name of any person or persons living or dead is purely coincidental.

INTRODUCTION

On 4 February 1966 Susan Read was admitted to St Bernard's mental hospital in Hanwell.

She was 12 years old. This is her book.

Sue is an imaginative woman who doesn't avoid extravagant language. Her story stretches credibility. Indeed it would be easy to dismiss the whole sorry tale as the fanciful ramblings of a lunatic or a liar. So we have appended the medical notes.

The record doesn't prove that Sue's contentions are accurate. In some ways they contradict her and certainly they redress the balance of her frequent condemnation of the doctors and others who were 'in charge' of her. Despite that, they imbue a credibility that cannot lightly be dismissed.

But, even if it were all true, it happened a long time ago. Surely psychiatric care must have improved immensely in the last 20 years? Hasn't the old mental hospital all but withered behind the flowering of community care? Sadly this is not so. Ward 19 looks and smells much as it did.

The dry documents are placed in an appendix that can be skipped; the reader is offered at once the red meat of Sue's account. Those whose interest lies in sensation, who wish to incite within themselves indignation and so condemn their fellow man, can read this book thus. They can go on to complain to their MP, join MIND, write to the newspapers.

It is equally possible to embrace the conservative role, to uphold the principles of decency, to realize that everyone did their best and that Miss Read was an obnoxious pest.

This is not a political treatise. Its aim is not to reform our psychiatric services. It has not been written as a one-woman

1

crusade to reform society. It is no more than Sue's story.

'No man is an island'; ask not who is responsible for the events these pages portray.

We all are.

Leslie Morrish

1

TRYING TO GROW

She always had a nap in the afternoon.

He had footsteps so loud they have a marked slot in my memory.

Was it only weekends and holidays that She took a nap, or all the time? I can't remember now, not like His footsteps.

Until recently I couldn't recall much of my childhood. I always felt we weren't allowed out to play. Why? Why did I feel this? Was it only sometimes? I shrug my shoulders; it doesn't matter now, does it?

Miss James was a woman who lived round several corners from us, in a filthy bungalow with lots of cats. She was so bent over, when you walked by, or called her, she had to move her whole body to the left or right to see you, exposing her screwed-up, wizened old face.

Miss James was a constant source of fun and games to us. We dared only to go into her kitchen. It was squalid. By the back door there was a cabinet, you know the kind, plastic patterned perspex sliding doors, pull-down front you cut your bread on, drawers underneath and wooden sliding doors. Inside the pull-down front were all sorts of salts, peppers, sugar, tea and spices. Every time we went there was a jelly and blancmange in rabbit moulds. We would carefully tip it out on to the pull-down front, salt it, pepper it, cut it all up and generally slosh it around making a yucky mess, then leave it and feed the birds with her bread.

I never once felt guilty, it was great fun. I was only seven years old. Pamela was 11 and Pauline was nearly six. They are my sisters. Sometimes David, the boy next door, came with us. He was 10.

The dump was a piece of wasteland with a tiny two-inch brook down the centre. I think I paddled, I'm not sure, but paddling would have been 'normal' so I presume I paddled.

The old lady with no legs lived near Miss James. I don't remember feeling guilty about our treatment of her, either. We would go blackberry-scrumping and bring them to her bungalow. She had bad eyesight and couldn't see the maggots crawling in and out as she ate them. 'Delicious, dears, thank you so much,' she'd say.

Her bungalow was smelly too. One day we took her a bundle of rhubarb we'd scrumped and she said she didn't like rhubarb. We each took a stick of rhubarb and beat her with it. Ungrateful old bag. No guilt again. Perhaps children don't feel guilty.

There was a little dog called Chummy, sweet thing, never bit anyone. Not just me, everyone would swing Chummy by the back legs over the church fence into the stinging nettles. Chummy would jump up and come back for more. It was fun — and still no guilt.

There were other times when I felt imprisoned in our house and garden. Pamela made up a game called feet-off-ground. There wasn't much to jump from, so it went something like this: board, bag, rags, tuft, tuft, slab, tuft, tuft. It was a good game.

The chairs in the kitchen were used as horses or covered and made into our camps. She always had a nap so we couldn't make a lot of noise.

I burned my pink jumper once by standing too close to the gas stove when a kettle was boiling. She was a good darner.

He sometimes helped me with my spelling. He would frighten me if I didn't know how to spell something and my mind would go blank. He wouldn't let us crunch crisps; we had to suck them until they were soggy. He hated Elvis Presley. One day Pamela plucked up courage and pushed a picture of Elvis under His nose. He threw His arms up and covered His eyes, in the same fashion Dracula would if confronted with a cross. I'm laughing now, it was so funny.

I remember once Pauline and I were sitting drawing. Pauline

was sitting closest to Him and for no reason He said, 'Sow it.'

Pauline turned to me and said, all sort of drawn out, 'See what I mean, Susan.'

She got a fat lip for that.

I hated the coal cellar. The thought of spiders. One night Pauline and I were messing around and not sleeping as we should have been. We were called down and grilled about 'Why you? When you? What you?' and then put in the coal cellar. Pauline loved it, she was a tomboy. She ran all over the coal, shrieking with delight. I was hysterical and screamed and screamed. He took Pauline out and left me in.

There are other incidents. They say it is fantasy. They love Him or prefer to feel they did. I didn't love Him, I was stark petrified of Him.

She was 42 when She had my brother Fred. I recall Her changing Fred on Her lap, while He was sitting at the table with the cup and saucer, milk and sugar and teapot beside Him. He only had to lift the teapot and pour, but He would flick His fingers and point to the teacup. She would leap up, clutching Fred to Her lap, and pour His tea. Everything for Him was flick, flick and point, and She leapt to it.

We didn't have a television; we didn't have much. He was tight with His money. He had a car. She struggled to keep the four of us fed and clothed. She was good. He was bad.

She said I hated Pauline, who was 21 months younger than me. I was a bit jealous but I didn't hate her.

He had a motor bike and side-car before Fred was born.

I must have been a horrible child. Every Christmas I would send my schoolfriends cards, put them in the red post-box we all helped to make, but I never got a card from anyone. This was in the Juniors. I don't remember the Infants.

One Christmas at home I got a red case with an umbrella attached. I must have been nine years old. I was running along the landing at 5.30 a.m. with the umbrella up and the case in my hand. I stopped outside His and Her bedroom and said, 'Piss.' Without warning the door opened and a hand flew out, bashed me and disappeared. I was stunned. I went back to bed. We didn't hear bad language at home except 'bloody' and 'sod'.

There was no love or physical affection between Him and Her or with us. No kisses and cuddles.

We took it in turns to get the pyjamas from the bottom of the stairs. I would argue like mad when my turn came. I was scared to death of going out there in the dark.

She taught me how to make beds and look after the house. I used to tuck Pauline into bed so that it would remain tidy, then I'd get into bed and make Pauline get up to put the light out, warning her not to wreck the bed.

He had a heart attack and was in Harrow Hospital for a number of weeks. I was 10, and began feeling unhappy and confused. I kept crying for no reason. She'd say, 'Don't turn on the waterworks.'

If I fell over and hurt myself I cried, or if He put me in the coal cellar I cried, but then I cried for nothing.

I kept saying over and over in my head that I was unhappy. The more I said it the more I cried, and the more I cried the unhappier I was. But why?

He came home from hospital. His bed was in the sitting-room. He took us upstairs very slowly. He was in the lead. He showed us how to pull the upstairs toilet chain.

'You pull it like this,' and He demonstrated.

'Not like this,' and He yanked it.

Slow procession of us going down the stairs, Him leading.

He had to take it easy because of His heart. He rushed about at work but He was painfully slow at home. He smoked like a trooper, and farted pointing His fingers to the light bulb.

I was unhappy and started wetting the bed and couldn't stop eating and drinking. She wouldn't let me drink because I was wetting the bed. He said I was doing it because Pauline wasn't putting the light on. I didn't wake up. Each morning my bed was wet.

I had an unbearable thirst and at school I drank the paint water. David's sister Diane told her mum and her mum told mine, and I was taken to the doctor. A month passed before I saw a consultant.

'Can you do a wee-wee, Susan?' said the doctor.

What a daft question. I was tired and my tummy hurt.

They gave me blood tests, wee tests, lots of tests. The doctor asked me to huff, and She said, 'Diabetes.' She had after all been a nurse.

I was admitted to Hillingdon Hospital and put in a room on my own. They put a drip in my arm and gave me injections in my bum. I can't remember minding awfully; I felt too ill the first couple of days.

I don't remember seeing Her, but His footsteps came every night.

He was about five feet nine inches tall, with a round face and a stocky build. He had a little hair round the back and a tiny fluffy bit on the top and often He had a moustache. I wasn't scared of Him in the hospital.

He didn't say anything but came every evening and looked at my chart. One evening He came earlier, and the nurse brought in the usual injection.

'Why don't you let Susan do it,' He said.

'We usually practise on an orange first,' said the nurse.

'No, Susan will do it, she'll have to do it when she comes home and for ever.'

I did the injection because He said, 'Do it.'

There were more injections. Two days after I started injecting myself I heard the words 'for ever'. When the footsteps came that evening, I asked what He meant and He explained. I didn't mind. I didn't realize.

I left the hospital. There was no special diet. He and She were horrified.

I was unhappier and cried more. If anyone was kind to me I felt confused. On March 30th He died. Pauline and I came home from school, and Mrs Perry opened the door to us. Looking through the kitchen window, I saw Her standing at the end of the washing-line.

'Your father is dead,' Mrs Perry said.

Pauline and I were sitting on the same chair by the porcelain sink, watching Her standing by the line.

'Are you going out to play?' Mrs Perry asked.

Why doesn't She come in, my head shouted, 'Come in here, I need you.'

She didn't come then, She didn't come ever.

I had diabetes. He was dead. She was lost.

2
ONLY FOR A FORTNIGHT

I changed from the Juniors to senior school, which I hated.

I hated the moving from class to class for different lessons. I was in the 'C' group.

At lunchtimes they made me sit at a table by myself away from all the other children. They gave me stupid dinners — stew with no potato, and baked apple. I hated it. They were frightened of my diabetes.

I felt lonely. None of my friends from the Juniors spoke to me; they thought I was trouble.

I soon found a way to make them notice me.

I was on my own in assembly, too. After a week of no one speaking to me, I was in assembly and I yelled out, 'Miss Chandler!'

'Yes, Read?'

'I think someone's shit, Miss, there's a dreadful smell — not you is it?'

There was an uproar. I was famous, all eyes on me from the top of the school to the bottom. Miss Chandler stood there, mouth wide open, so taken aback she dismissed assembly, me included.

I went to the class where I was due. The girls were all rowdy and invited me to join in; I didn't need to be asked twice. It was great fun, throwing books, slamming desks, snapping pencils. When the teacher came in, I got caught. Everyone else was sitting like goodie two-shoes.

'Read, what are you doing?'

'Don't you know, it isn't just me, they were as well.'

'Read, sit down.'

'Christ,' I hissed and flopped down.

They decided I was a disruptive influence on the school and would be suspended, pending a decision on what to do about me.

I then spent my days at home with Her. While She went to Quack Waddie's to clean his flat, I stayed at home and cleaned our house. I loved ironing and washing the red-tiled floor in the kitchen.

In a dish on his dressing-table Quack Waddie had a tiny black doll about two inches tall, dressed in beads. Every time She dared to take me there I would sit on his bed, holding the tiny doll, looking into the dressing-table mirror, thinking of nothing. When Quack Waddie moved away he gave me that dolly. For some reason the need for her disappeared once I had her. I used to long for her, but once I had her it didn't matter.

The paraffin man would call on our neighbourhood every Saturday evening. He was short, 36ish, had a cockney accent and was very bandy. I would take the paraffin to the customers and collect the money. She didn't like it; She said it was wrong hanging around with men and talking indecent. 'Wouldn't do this if your father was alive,' She'd nag.

I wasn't allowed to talk to the paraffin man because it wasn't 'done'. What wasn't done, I would ask myself. She told me years later that he would talk dirty.

Any man who talked to me was wrong and would talk dirty. I seemed to attract this kind of sexual interest.

I was the baker's girl for a year before I got diabetes. Every Saturday morning, come rain or shine, I would go and meet him and help to deliver the bread until the end of his round, which was my road. I knew that round as well as he did. The baker had corned-beef sandwiches in a Tupperware box for his lunch and a thermos of coffee which he shared with me. He would say, 'Come on, Sue, warm your hands on the cup.' When it was cold he would cuddle me in the front of his van.

I would hang around the paraffin man, not helping him. She kept saying it was wrong. She wouldn't leave me alone; She followed me everywhere I went. If I went to the park She came along. She was my shadow.

I'd say, 'Fuck off,' and She would clap Her hand to Her mouth and gasp. So I would scream, 'Fuck off!' all long and drawn out. Everyone was horrified.

One day I showed the paraffin man my knickers and made sure She saw me do it.

Once I came home from the park and had an insulin reaction. Mr Chilton from next door had to come in and hold me still for Her to administer sugar.

All the time She would say to Pam, Pauline and Fred, 'Now don't start her off, just leave her alone,' as if I wasn't there.

So I would shout, 'I can't get the fucking bubbles out!'

'Ssh, leave her,' She would say. Not a sound. Everyone would go deaf and dumb.

'Is someone going to get these fucking bubbles out or not?' I'd grab Fred and pretend to inject him. All hell would break loose. Mr Hill, Mr Chilton, half the men in the neighbourhood were called in to restrain me, an 11-year-old kid weighing about five and a half stone.

I ran into the toilet and locked the door, smashed the syringe and let them panic for a while. I read a few comics — Pam always kept a good supply in the loo — then I opened the door and came out. After that and to this day there is no lock on the loo door.

Strangely enough, I missed school; I got bored and didn't know what to do with myself.

She had promised Him before He died to transfer me from Hillingdon to Hammersmith Hospital where I was born. Apparently they had a good diabetic clinic.

The clinic was on a Friday morning. I would tantalize Her in the train on the journey there. I'd lift up Her skirt and say to the men in the carriage, 'What d'you think of these legs? Don't you reckon they're sexy?'

Same old junk every time I went. Stick your finger in a bowl of water, then let them stick a pin in it to get a fasting blood sugar, then into a cubicle to do your injection and wait for three to four hours.

Breakfast was a cup of tea and home-made egg sandwiches. They stank to high heaven, giving me the chance to show Her up yet again. 'Who's farted?' I'd call out loudly.

I always came away from there having said or done something obnoxious for an 11-year-old. They would sit and watch me push and provoke Her. They pretended I wasn't there when they weren't gasping in horror. Again I felt so confused that I cried.

She told me that at one stage I went to a school for maladjusted children because I 'had to be at school'. I had only been there a week when one day after the teacher told me off I went to the cloakroom, took all the coats from their pegs, put them in the middle of the washroom floor and flooded it. Needless to say, after that I didn't go to school any more. I don't remember that or other incidents I have mentioned; I am explaining them through Her telling me. I feel sure they are significant.

After a while She told Dr Melvin at Hammersmith Hospital that my behaviour was bad. She explained all the incidents (very thorough She was). Dr Melvin said that His having died, followed by the diabetes and then puberty on its way, was probably the cause of the problems.

She said, 'No, it's more than that. She swears, threatens Fred with her syringe, she does, she's uncontrollable, she is. Something has to be done; we're all suffering, we are.'

'Hello Susan, or will I call you Sue? I'm Dr Hersov. I'm here to help you.'

'Help me do what, get better from diabetes?'

'No, nothing like that, something different. We'll leave your mum here and go into my office.'

I remember feeling a distinct hatred for Dr Hersov on that first meeting. He was thumbing through notes, watching me at the same time. 'Tell me about yourself, Sue.'

I stayed silent. There was a round plastic ball with different shapes, and he said, 'Sue, are you clever enough, I wonder, to know which shapes go into which hole?'

'Stupid berk.'

'Do you like making sand-castles, Sue?'

'I've never made one.'

'Surely you did, Sue, when you were a little girl at the seaside.'

'Didn't go to the seaside.'

'But everyone goes to the seaside.'

'Well I bleeding well didn't. You're fucking barmy.'

His face went all red as if it would explode. 'That's enough for today, I will see you next week. Goodbye.'

'Good fucking riddance,' I mumbled.

'Mummy he's nuts, he thinks I'm stupid. He told me to see if I was clever enough to put toys in the holes. Why should I do that, Mum? Tell him I'm clever. I hate him, he's creepy and fucking ugly.'

'Now Shue, he wants to help you, he does, to find out why you cry and why you're naughty. Come on now, don't start swearing, let's go home just this once without swearing.'

'All right Mum.' I liked Her when She acted as though She knew I could be nice. Feet-off-ground, don't tread on the cracks in the pavement, and we walked in step like soldiers all the way to East Acton station.

I hadn't been to school for months. I hadn't been anywhere except Hammersmith.

I don't remember seeing Dr Hersov more than twice, but the second time he made me put the round dollies inside one another. They were wooden and wobbly.

'Do you know anything about sex, Sue?'

'Of course I do.' I smiled; he was on my favourite subject.

'What do you know? Have you done it?'

I could feel he was nervous. 'Of course.'

'Do you like babies?'

'Yes, I love them, I'm going to have one . . . one day. I haven't.'

'Haven't what?'

'Had it off, stupid.'

'Why do you keep talking about sex and swearing? You appear to know quite a lot.'

'Fucking idiot.' I remember thinking how stupid I was to get into these conversations. 'I know nothing mate, so just piss off and leave me alone.' With that I picked up the wooden wobbly dollies and threw them at him. 'Piss off.'

I went outside and sat beside Her. I don't know a lot after

that, but She was cross and wouldn't talk to me on the way home or for some time after.

I don't like being ignored, so when the time came to do my injection I drew up my insulin and smashed the syringe on to the wooden draining-board. 'That's that, no more of them, see if I care. You don't have to talk to me, shitbag.'

Ssh, don't say a word, leave her alone, let her get on with it, don't upset her. They all go deaf and dumb again.

I can't understand, and cry again.

Why do I do these things? Why does my head feel so different to how it did a long time ago? He didn't help me, that Hersov, I felt he hated me like I hated him, stupid fucking bastard.

Next morning, there was my syringe; everything was as if it had never happened. Nobody upset me and I didn't upset them. They didn't because they were warned not to; I didn't because it sometimes took a lot of energy to start something, and I didn't fancy starting what I couldn't continue. I was always unhappy and bored.

She related a particular story to me that put the lid on it, so to speak.

Pauline and I went out, and later Pauline arrived home frantic without me, saying I had gone into a hut with two or three workmen. She went off next door for Mr Chilton. Pauline and She got into his car and came to do a Batman rescue.

'Imagine if Pauline hadn't had the common sense to come and fetch me, imagine. You'd have been raped and murdered, you would.' She was nearly hysterical.

I don't remember that incident, but I can say not one of the workmen touched me and I didn't encourage them to. I do remember feeling only a little girl when apparently I was actively encouraging rape and murder among innocent men.

'Come on, Shue.' She always whistled as if there was an 'h' in Sue. 'We are going to see a doctor who might be able to help you get into school.'

'Goodie.'

The special schools wouldn't have me because of the

diabetes; they didn't have the facilities to cope with it. The diabetic boarding schools wouldn't have me because of the problems.

I wasn't quite the ticket.

'She's not quite the ticket,' they'd all say, with their lips puckered up making a sucking sound. Doesn't explain anything positive or negative.

'I'm going to see a doctor who's going to get me into school and help me find out why I'm unhappy and cry, goodie, goodie,' I told myself often over the next few days.

I can't remember whether we went by car or by bus but I vividly remember arriving.

It looked like miles and miles of brick wall, 10 feet tall brick wall. There was a huge brick arch with iron gates that were open. The arch was covered in ivy. To the right of this arch was a sort of sentry box. She spoke to the man and he talked away, making movements with his arms.

We walked to the end of the road with trees on both sides. We turned right just before the church with a clock, and a little further on we turned left. Along this road there was mud and bushes to your right, and on your left a high brick wall, a huge building with small windows, eight tiny panes in each one. This building seemed to stretch for miles.

When we got to the ward there were two huge doors, but we only opened one. Directly ahead was a waiting area. Sister told us to sit there. We did.

We waited and waited. Christ how I hated having to wait. So I began to create. 'Where is this stupid doctor, what is this place? I'm hungry, I shall be hypo, give me something to eat, I'm sick of waiting,' I whined.

'Ssh, Susan, don't make things worse, come on now, be sensible, it won't be much longer now, it won't,' She pleaded.

I was in an awkward mood and I wouldn't be sensible.

In the end I saw the doctor and straight away I knew he was another Hersov. While he talked to Her I had to go and wait outside. Then we went home. I don't remember any more, but about a week later I was told to pack some things; I was going to stay somewhere else for a while.

We were back at the arch covered in ivy. We went through the one door of Ellis Ward where we had been before.

'It's only for a fortnight, Shue, until we can find something better. Just to give Mummy a rest, it is.'

She kissed my forehead and went.

3

THE OAK TREE

I was in this place for a fortnight. I ticked off the days. (For a fortnight.) I was there for about 24 hours before I realized it was a mental home. 'St Bernard's Hospital', it said in huge white letters on the ivy-covered arch. I was in Ellis Ward. It was a large dormitory; there were about 30 beds with lockers beside them and loos at the end to your right.

To the left was a little room with four beds along one wall. Ellis Ward wasn't a bad place to be; people didn't seem too mental. I remember asking the Sister what people who were mental looked like, because in Ellis they all looked ordinary, 'like me'.

'Well, there's your answer Susan,' she said. I laughed and rushed off.

I know there was a padded cell in Ellis, because I played in it when I had the chicken-pox. At first they thought I had German measles, and there was a pregnant lady in Ellis, so they asked me if I minded staying in the padded cell if they left the door open. I didn't mind, it was good fun. I was in there for about three days. I got a stye on my left eye; it was painful.

There was a lady called Peggy in Ellis Ward who was 40ish. There didn't seem anything wrong with her, but when her husband came to pick her up for the weekend she would cry and cry, and when she came back she was as happy as a sandgirl.

The Sister in charge was called Sister Selby. She was tall with dark hair, slim, and would have been attractive if she hadn't been so hard-faced. They thought they were going to do my insulin injections, but I wouldn't let them; I'd been doing them myself for a year with no trouble. They didn't like

17

me doing it, so every injection time we had a row. 'I'm a hospital Sister you know, I'm not your mother. Don't you think you can do as you like here.'

Sister would prod and poke me around. She would call me a nasty little guttersnipe. Because I wanted to inject myself they made life pretty difficult for me when they could find time.

Sometimes I would wander off somewhere to find something to do. The place was huge; once out of Ellis Ward I nearly got lost a number of times. I made a firm friend of a 50ish woman named Freda, who would tell me lots of things about God. She would say I was the little girl with the little curl in the middle of her forehead. Freda liked me and I liked her. I believe she eventually died there.

Mum would sometimes come to see me on a Tuesday afternoon.

'Can I come home, Mum?'

'Not yet, Shue.'

'But why? I promise I'll be good.'

'Shue, your promises don't last long. Stay now and be good until they make you better.'

'But Mum I don't feel ill. Did you know this is a nut-house, Mum?'

I watched her face and she went all odd. 'No, no of course it isn't, it's just an ordinary hospital. It says so at the gate now, doesn't it.'

'I suppose so.' I didn't know what to say.

There was a woman called Mrs Farr from the League of Friends who would bring Mum and then take her home again.

That fortnight was going on eight weeks when they kept threatening to put me in 19s if I didn't toe the line. I would get bored then I would provoke the other patients or wander off for hours. Usually I sat by the big oak tree by the canal and picked buttercups to make a daisy chain. When I got back they would go on and on at me to tell them where I had been. The more they went on the less I would say; after all, I hadn't been doing anything wrong.

Selby would say, 'I'm going to get great pleasure in sending you to 19s.

'What's 19s?' I would ask.

'You just wait.'

'How the bleeding hell can you scare me when I don't know what 19s is? Have you got a coal cellar?'

She laughed and I laughed. She never knew what I meant and I never knew what she meant.

Dr Blair was the doctor Mum had spoken to the week before I went in there. He was of middle height, balding, and wore a dark brown suit with a shiny backside. He smoked cigars and kept looking at his watch while smiling smarmily, pretending to be interested in what you were telling him. I hated him. He smelt dreadful, like something from a jumble sale, all musty and sweaty. He was Hersov but was called Blair.

When I was at home before Dad died we never had a bath. We sat on the draining-board with our feet in the washing-up bowl. I sat on one side and Pauline sat on the other. Until I left there we bathed that way. I can't remember having a bath on Ellis or anyone saying I smelt. I suppose I washed at the sink; that's what I was used to. I didn't like cleaning my teeth.

I liked Sunday school and the little pink dress below my knees with a thick sash tapering off into a thin belt around my waist. It was covered in tiny red roses. I loved it. Sunday school was nice; there were tiny wooden chairs to sit on. I would listen to the stories with Pauline and the other children. Joseph's coat of many colours was my favourite. At one stage they gave each child a picture book about the life of Jesus. I wanted to give that book to my own children but I can't find it now.

I was about seven years old when Dad put me in his red van and took me to see Nanny Read. She was short and plump with white hair. She wore an apron which was worn over the shoulders and tied at the sides, with one long pocket in the front.

I don't remember other times seeing Nanny Read, but this visit stays vivid. She was standing waiting by the front gate, and she took my hand and led me into her house. She told

Dad to sit me on the chair, which he did. I had to sit very still and quiet.

When we left she put her hand into her apron pocket and took out a little purse, which she rummaged in for what seemed like ages; then she gave me a silver sixpenny piece (a tanner), took my face in both her hands and kissed my cheek.

'Goodbye.'

'Bye-bye, Nanny Read.'

On the way home I told Dad I would never ever spend the sixpence or wash Nanny's kiss off my cheek. He raised his eyebrows. When we got home I heard the ice-cream man outside. I rushed out and bought a sixpenny cornet. I really enjoyed it. When I went indoors, Mum saw my face was covered in ice-cream. She took a face flannel and washed it off. I cried bitterly.

'Whatever is wrong with you, Shue?'

'You've washed Nanny's kiss off my cheek.' It never occurred to me that I had spent her sixpence. Nanny Read was still alive when Dad died.

I never met Nanny Smith. When she died, Mum went to Wales for the funeral. She left us all with a neighbour, whose house was manky. Pauline, Pam and I slept in a double bed. When we asked for a drink the lady gave us a dirty cup of water from the bathroom tap. There were lots of drinking-chocolate bottles in the bath, and scum so thick the bath looked slimline.

I only went to Wales once (my mum was born and bred there), but I vividly recollect what happened while I was there. If I stood in the centre of the road, facing me the road was very steep, also to the left and right; like three steep hills. Behind me the road was flat and to my right was a little park, and just before the park was my Aunt Madge's house, all on its own with a short wall round it. I ventured up the road singing 'Jack and Jill went up the hill'. There were houses on both sides. When I got to the top I fell, just like in the nursery rhyme. My mum verifies this memory by saying the surroundings I described are correct. It's a long way back in my mind's eye.

We were allowed to go penny-for-the-guy and carol-singing. We used to make a fortune. We lived near an American air base, and the Yanks never could resist my little sister, Pauline. They'd say, 'Ain't she cute,' because she wore National Health glasses and a patch over one eye. Pauline nearly always got five shillings a time.

Susan up the road was my best friend. She knew everything I didn't. I sort of admired her. She had waist-length platinum-blonde hair, a beautiful face and a doting mother and father. Her dad would do anything for her. He took her to school round the corner after doing his night-shift. He idolized her.

Susan would kick me in the ankles when I stood in assembly with my feet all twisted round each other. She wouldn't tell me what 'an old jalopy' meant; I really never knew. When I was nine she told me about babies and monthlies; she scared me half to death. I remember looking at my mum and dad and all yucky thoughts were in my head. I thought, they did that and then we came. They were beasts.

Susan told me that when people died they looked really scary, all wide-eyed and staring; their eyes would never close and they would haunt you. She said my dad looked like that now he was dead. On the day of Dad's funeral, Mum brought his body home. I told her what Susan had said. She went off somewhere and then asked Pauline and me if we wanted to see Dad. I was petrified.

We went into the living-room and there lay my father. He appeared very young-looking, no wrinkles, no frowns either. I stood and looked at him in his coffin and said to myself, 'Never again will I be afraid of anyone.'

We all went to the church and listened to what the vicar said. Pam went with Mum to the cemetery. Pauline and I went back and stayed with Mrs Poole until they all returned. We watched Pam and Mum go off. We stood outside the church, then put our arms around each other and cried, then broke away and ran back to Mrs Poole at number 5.

It was Easter time. Aunt Betty came to Dad's funeral and stayed overnight with her little girl, who was three years old. I had three Easter eggs. I gave her two, and when she'd eaten them she started screaming. Aunt Betty came and slapped me across the face, accusing me of hurting her child. She wouldn't listen to my explanation — not that I had one, I didn't know what was happening. My face hurt like mad and my pride hurt worse, so I called her a 'fucking cow'. My mum wouldn't talk to me, I was always so naughty. At the end of that day I had a tremendous feeling of freedom.

Pam got a letter saying she could start work at BEA.

I did feel guilty when I was told it was my fault that Pauline was called a St Bernard dog at school and didn't have a friend in the whole place because her sister was a mental case.

Pam came to visit me almost every Thursday, when there was a social evening. Pam would take me to the social. It was held on Ellis. I loved it; at the age of 12 I could waltz, foxtrot, and cha-cha like Valentino. Two men called Tom and Bill would bring in their tape recorder and give us two hours of social evening. Half-way through, one of the patients would make refreshments — tea that was like axle grease and Rich Tea biscuits like balsa wood.

Once when Mum came to see me on Ellis she mentioned that my teeth were yellow. 'Almost orange they are.' She then asked for a second opinion (she still does it even now) from Sister Selby, saying. 'Does Susan clean her teeth? Would you not say they were disgusting?'

'Jesus Christ, all right, I'll clean my bleeding teeth.' I proceeded to go through the motions of cleaning my teeth with my finger, making revolting squeaky noises.

Sister exploded, '19s, 19s, I've had enough of your cheek, 19s for you.'

At that I turned and ran as fast as I could through Ellis and out of the back door. The pregnant lady and Peggy ran after me. The pregnant one fell over; unaware, I carried on running. I had nearly reached the gate when the giant-sized nurse chasing me called to a nurse in front and she caught me. Between them they hauled me back to Sister.

'You wouldn't have got out,' she yelled. 'I'd rung the gate

and he would have stopped you. 19s for you, 19s for you.' If she said '19s for you' once she said it 20 times.

I still didn't know what 19s was even when I packed my things ready. Mum said she would come with me.

Selby was mooching around like a demented parrot. She was delighted I was going to 19s. I guessed that as she had a permanent smile, she ought to have come with me.

Two nurses built like houses, Mum and I set off to the dreaded 19s. Bloody long walk it was, right into the main building, four storeys high and no lifts. We trudged up four flights of stairs, then through ward after ward. Each door was unlocked, then locked again. We got to 19s in the end and one of the nurses banged on the door. We had to wait for ages before anyone came.

The nurse who opened the door had a bunch of keys on the end of a chain tied securely at her waist. She turned the key once to the left, then to the right and then to the left again; the main door was triple-locked.

'This is 19s? It looks like a Wendy house,' I said aloud.

The nurses who came with us went to the office with the nurse who had opened the door, leaving Mum and me standing there. A thin, scraggy woman tottered over to my mum and said, 'You'll be all right here, dear. I'm a lesbian and her over there killed her mum and dad. You'll be all right, love.'

My mum went to pieces. The story as I heard it later was that Mum left there and went straight to the head of the hospital, saying she wasn't having her daughter left in there. I would have to be removed.

I have no recollection whatsoever of my two days spent at 19s for the crime of cleaning my teeth with my fingers. I do know that I was soon back on Ellis, with cranky Sister Selby prodding me around.

I hated that woman vehemently.

4

US

'You never talk to me, you never take any responsibilities in this dump. I fucking hate you, you leave it all to me,' I scream at my husband Stephen.

All I seem to do these days is shout and scream. I know he works hard for a pittance, but I work hard too. I look after this dump, I look after his child and his responsibilities, I cook and clean and do all the mundane things 'just a housewife' does, and go out to work in the evening. God damn him, why doesn't he talk to me?

We've been married 18 months. Our daughter Sheryl Nicole is six months old. We live in a three-bedroomed house with lounge, dining-room, kitchen and bathroom. Things between us were lovely before we moved here, but the council wouldn't let us stay in our flat with a child. The rent is three times higher than it was at the flat. The heating system is ridiculous; there are air vents over the doors in every room except two bedrooms. We can't afford to run it.

I clean at the local hospital. It's a 15-hour week, 6 p.m. to 9 p.m. I hate going out when Steve comes home, but we need the money. He puts Sheryl to bed, and I see to her nappies when I come home. I get up at 7 a.m. I look after Sheryl, do all my housework and paint toy soldiers for a pittance, and still go to work in the evening.

I must sort myself out before Sheryl gets any older. I want her to grow into a normal young woman. I don't want her head to be in constant turmoil like mine. She is bright and beautiful, the best child any mother could wish for. We also have a golden Labrador called Bruce.

Steve is five feet nine inches tall, handsome, and has dark

curly hair. He is kind and generous, but introvert. I admit I find this aspect of our marriage frustrating. I'm five feet seven inches tall, sharp-featured, and have fine blonde hair. I weigh eight and a half stone, which is good; diabetics have a tendency to obesity. My nature isn't very nice. I'm kind enough until someone upsets me; then I'm nasty, physically and verbally. I have never smacked Sheryl. I've shouted until I'm hoarse, but I haven't spanked her.

Bruce is growling; he thinks someone is at the gate. Shut up Bruce.

It's 5.20 p.m. I have to be at work at 6 p.m. and I haven't changed Sheryl or done my hair. Bruce is snuggling up; all right, I'll feed you in a minute.

I haven't got any money for dinner again today. I went down to the heap but there weren't any vegetables there. What am I going to do? Sheryl and I are ravenous. Never mind, she's had her milk.

Today was spent at the Lister out-patients about my diabetes. I've got these painful red lumps on my legs. They used some medical jargon I can't spell let alone pronounce. The lumps look revolting, but they say I won't die, so hard luck.

I tend to be a bit of a pest. I even get on my own nerves.

My hands are red raw too. Shut up, Susan, you sound like a hypochondriac.

On Monday I have a new cooker being delivered. I'm thrilled to bits. (Small things please small minds.)

My kitchen floor is filthy. Susan, it needs a good scrubbing. The house needs hoovering; Bruce is moulting and his hair gathers in the corners of the room like tumbleweed. The wretched house is like a hovel. I'm being a bore; even a machine gets time off.

The temperature here is below freezing and my head is all screwed up. Bastard bleeding thoughts. Here I am telling myself something I know already, and does it work? No, not for me. I mustn't cry, it's wrong. I must be hard, even when it isn't working out.

I really believed when I started that I could get my fears and tensions on to paper and it would be all right. Now I'm sobbing with anger, the tension in my throat is unbearable and my stomach is heaving. It's so tight inside. I need someone to help me. I feel so desperate, so frightened for myself and my baby.

I wouldn't care about the tension if it wasn't so apparent to everyone. My throat muscles are moving involuntarily all the time. I feel disgusted for getting to such a pitch. Nothing works. I take Valium, I talk to people and scream and shout, yet it's still there.

I wish I'd been born without a brain; then I wouldn't have to endure these thoughts that persecute me. Please help me. I feel close to taking my life. If I die, then Sheryl comes with me; I won't leave her behind. My stomach heaves when I go to eat.

If I had loads and loads of crockery, or panes and panes of glass, I'd smash and smash and smash until there wasn't one piece left intact. I'd beat something, tear things to pieces, punch my fists, my head. I want to run and run and when I get to Land's End to jump to death. How I pray for peace of mind.

I feel calmer now, even though the tension is still there. I can smell a stew I'm cooking; my stomach heaves.

Susan you shouldn't smoke so much — 60 fags a day, frequently more. I wake in the morning and first thing is a fag.

Susan you're disgusting.

Steve said dinner smells good. He cut himself shaving. I kissed him. Steve and I rarely kiss. I wish he wasn't so wary about affection. I've told him how much I want him to hold me close, but he thinks it's silly. Bruce lie down.

Steve takes the mickey out of my throat tension, and that hurts me. I tell him I feel he can't love me if he can't sympathize, and he'll say, 'Don't be mad,' and then we — or rather I — argue and he sits and glares. I am so unhappy, so confused and very frightened. Sheryl is crying. I hate myself for not having any patience with her.

Steve made love to me last night. He hasn't for three months and I have missed him dreadfully. I cried, because I felt happy, and the tension went away for a short time. Steve I love you so much.

Steve earned some money today for taking someone to Heathrow Airport. We had a disagreement before he left and I said I hoped he crashed the van and killed himself. I worried the whole time he was out. My emotions change so quickly from love to hate.

Susan you're a callous bitch, you really must check yourself.

I'm all mixed up. I'll take another Valium and get a good night's sleep. I CAN'T SLEEP. I'm too tense.

What will become of this stupid farce called our marriage?

I love my baby. Tonight before putting her to bed I held her in my arms and loved her with all the tenderness I could muster, and she never struggled to be released.

Today again I feel calm. I have had my new cooker delivered and must wash the kitchen floor. I've been playing with Sheryl. I love to hear her shriek with laughter and ramble 'ma ma da da'.

Someone came today and saw me writing, and asked if I was a writer.

'No, just a nutcase,' I said.

Why did they let me out of St Bernard's? There are lots of days when I feel as if I've really lost my sanity. The tension is unbearable. I wish I was back in St Bernard's. I didn't have to do things like care or even think in there.

I wish I was back in St Bernard's.

5

MY NAME WAS JENNY

Ward 19 was locked. It annoyed me that I couldn't get out. I wanted to sit under the oak tree. I would get terrific longings to run. There was nowhere in 19s I could go to be in private; even the toilets had saloon-type swing-doors.

After I'd been admitted to 19s they showed me to my bed, which was inside the door of the dormitory on the right. Sister's office was outside the dormitory doors on the left. The dormitory had approximately 40 beds, with lockers beside them. They were in rows of four, six beds to a row. Against the wall were five rooms, each with a panel of wired glass in the door. These rooms could be double-locked. Inside there was only a bed and jerry. If you walked past my bed to the end of the dormitory there were two toilets to be used at night. I never used them; there were always loud breathing noises and an awful smell in there.

My first friend in 19s was Sylvia. Poor Sylvia was pathetic. She spent nine months out of 12 in the PR (padded cell).

Sylvia was five feet four inches tall, with mousey-coloured hair which hung lank and greasy round her neck. She was slim and walked as though she had her best foot forward. Neither staff nor patients liked Sylvia. She was violent. She had sad eyes that looked sleepy, and her bottom lip drooped. If she spoke too fast she dribbled. I wasn't scared of Sylvia. I sort of loved and looked after her. She was 19.

I had been in 19s for three weeks when this girl ran towards me shouting, 'Jen, Jenny.' She flung her arms around me, squeezing me tight.

I was scared. I pushed her away.

'Jenny, it's Sylvia.' Sylvia thought I was her little sister Jenny.

That was our first meeting and we were inseparable thereafter. When Sylvia was in the PR she wouldn't eat. She would call, 'Jenny, Jenny.' I was allowed to sit in the PR with her; we spent hours together in there. The nurses didn't come in with me; they would open the door push me in and slam it shut.

Sylvia was illiterate. She couldn't write her own name. She stuttered badly. I taught her to write her name and the name she called me — Jenny. She learnt to write 'cat' and 'dog' and other words — not a lot, but for her it was wonderful.

Sylvia wasn't allowed to have a mattress or ticking blankets. In theory, when in the PR you were safe from yourself. Not Sylvia. She would tear the ticking to shreds, throw the jerry up to the light until the bulb broke and then cut herself up. She cut her nipples off and swallowed them. She straightened out wire coat-hangers and inserted them into her bellybutton. She pushed them into her vagina and back passage and pulled. She cut the corners of her eyes, mouth and ear lobes. Her whole body was scarred — not little cuts, but deep gashes.

When Sylvia was in the pads she had nothing. She had to do her toilet down the gully. Her pad wasn't cleaned until she came out. The smell was terrible; my stomach turned for weeks.

Some days Sylvia wouldn't talk and I would be unhappy. She'd slap my face, then kiss my cheek. I hated it when Sylvia didn't talk to me. On those days I didn't go in the pads.

For two days I hadn't seen Sylvia. When I went into the pads, there on the wall, written in her own mess, were 'Sylvia' and 'Jenny'. The words were scrawled, but she had tried so hard. I cuddled and kissed her. Poor Sylvia was covered in excrement. The smell was vile, but I didn't care; that day Sylvia was beautiful. I had a feeling of awakening towards her.

One night I was lying awake in bed and I wondered whether Sylvia had pains. She never seemed to feel anything. Next time I was in the pads with her, I gently ran my fingers round her face, tracing the scars. She wanted to write and brushed me away. 'Doog', she wrote.

'No, Sylvie. Dog, only one "o". I'd taught her how to

pronounce it. D-O-G. She would say 'D-O-O-G' because she stuttered. She slapped my face. She always hit me when she couldn't do something. I ran my fingers over her tummy and nippleless breasts. She brushed me away.

There was another girl called Susan, for whom I harboured such a hatred it was scary. She was cruel and despicable. She attacked other patients and destroyed their belongings. She had a maimed leg. The cause came out in different versions: once she said she had jumped out of a 10th-storey window; another time she said she had leapt out of a car travelling at 70 m.p.h. She and Sylvia were always kissing. Every opportunity Susan got she'd hit or kick me. If Sylvia caught her she would give her a good hiding, for which she was sent back in the pads.

It didn't make sense. They were always kissing, yet if Susan touched me, Sylvia would beat her up.

When I was pregnant with Sheryl, I met Susan in Shepherd's Bush market. She said she'd married Terry, one of the inmates I knew when I was there. They seemed quite happy, even though they kept contradicting each other. She kept repeating like a parrot, 'When are you coming home, Jenny?'

Everyone got up at 6 a.m. There was a rota. The floors had to be washed and polished. Every bed was made by its occupant. The ward was cleaned every day. I found it hard to manage the big industrial polishers because I was only five stone 11 pounds. I could barely put the wax on with the huge bumper; I'd try to escape doing the polishing and attempt to wax instead. I learnt early on, if you looked busy in 19s you were left alone. To be different from the majority was fatal. I didn't mind the work but it was so heavy I couldn't manage.

The patients kept the ward clean under strict supervision. If you stopped working to pick your nose or scratch your arse you were slapped or kicked. I would be waxing the floor when Nurse Benson, a bleached blonde, fat and ugly bitch, would tell me she was a cow. 'Susan, will I tell you?'

'Tell me what, nurse?'

'I'm a cow. What am I?'

'Don't know.'

With the back of her hand she flat-punched my face. 'I told you, I'm a cow. What am I, Susan?' She'd hit me again. 'Come on, you daft-looking fucker, tell me what I am.'

'Cow, cow, you're a cow,' I'd scream.

Then I'd get the full treatment.

Every day Benson hit me and kicked me and made me call her a cow so she could hit and kick me some more. In the end I learnt how to master the huge polisher and waxing bumper. Sheer anger taught me.

When all the cleaning was done we'd have breakfast. Winnie and Minnie had been in 19s for 25 years, so they'd lay the tables and fill the teapots and marmalade pots at each meal. There were four people to each table. I never specifically sat at any one table.

When the breakfast trolley arrived, which a patient and nurse fetched, everyone sat down. Winnie and Minnie then wheeled the two-tier trolley along the aisle between the locked rooms and the tables and put four forks, four knives, four cups and saucers, one pot of marmalade, a plate with four slices of toast, one teapot, one jug of milk and a basin of sugar on each table. As there were between 60 and 65 patients on 19s, including the violent ones in locked rooms, the food by the time it reached us was little short of swill. They served the patients in the rooms first and there were usually 20 — more if it was a bad week. But like my brain, my stomach learnt to accept anything.

After the meals there was the cutlery-counting. It drove me round the twist. It would take anything up to an hour, depending on whether or not some bright spark had decided to hide a knife or fork on their person; if so, then everyone except Minnie and the staff sat at the tables until the numbers were correct. Then — until the next meal — the time was your own, to do with what you liked.

There wasn't anything to do. All the cleaning was already done. Sometimes I would curl up in a chair, but there weren't enough chairs for everyone. I would try to go to sleep, but either Sister would yell at me to get up (sleeping in the day was forbidden) or someone would grab me by the scruff of my neck and seize the chair for themselves. Then there I was again, fed up, knocked about and hankering for trouble. Even deep trouble was better than nothing in 19s.

I learnt that if you went on the rounds with a nurse you were privileged and exempt from polishing and waxing. Every day for nearly a month I would ask Sister Dickinson if I could go on the rounds. Each time I asked she boxed my ears, but in the end I won. She got me by the ear and said, 'Now you can go on the rounds, but if I hear one wrong thing, woe betide you,' and she boxed my ears again.

It was hard work on the rounds (sometimes I thought harder than polishing). The nurse and I would leave the ward at 9.30 a.m. There was a barrow about three feet long, with an upside-down-U-shaped handle, which I had to push around to various places. On top of the barrow was a crate of empty milk bottles. Each ward had to be unlocked and then relocked, until we got to the lift. Then it was down to the ground floor and along a corridor to turn left into the kitchen area. There I would leave the crate of empty bottles.

We would visit the pharmacy and collect the pills and plasters. The medicine was in a 10-inch by 10-inch metal box with a tiny padlock. Then we'd go on to the laundry, where we'd pick up bundles of sheets, pillowcases, blankets, nighties and rough striped dressing-gowns that chafed your skin. Next stop was the post office to collect the mail, then back to the kitchen to pick up a crate of milk.

All this took until 11 a.m., maybe 11.15 if I dawdled — which I did more often than not. This was the highlight of my day. My back ached for the first week, but soon I didn't notice minor things like backache.

Jean had been in St Bernard's for 26 years because she had epilepsy. She had been adopted when she was a baby, and she idolized this woman she referred to as 'my adopted mummy'.

Jean was well-spoken and seemed to come from a good background. I was a foul-mouthed little bitch, and whenever I swore Jean would make a point of telling me how unladylike this was.

Once a week Jean got dressed in her best clothes, applied thick red lipstick, dabbed powder on her face and took great pains to let everyone know she was off to see her 'adopted mummy'. This was a ritual that annoyed me after a while. She would come back happy and elated, with a small gift from her 'adopted mummy', and would prattle on about her delightful day out to anyone who would listen. Her 'adopted mummy' never came to 19s; Jean always went out for the day — but never for a weekend, nor for Christmas. I wondered if her 'adopted mummy' really existed. Even at the age of 13 it all seemed like a charade.

I was particularly bored one day after being thrown out of my chair, and there was Jean dolled up in her best clothes, her face surrounded in a cloud of face powder, and wearing that red lipstick. I mimicked her, saying, 'I'm going out for an utterly splendid day with my adopted mummy.' I spoke as Jean did, as though I had a plum in my mouth.

She glared at me, but even after I had repeated myself with a few variations, she refused to rise to the bait. I then said to her, 'I suppose your dear old "adopted mummy" wouldn't dream of coming here to see you in a nut-house.'

Jean turned on me, raising her hand level with my head, then dropped it, stamped her feet and stormed out of the dormitory. I felt good. I was bored; there was never anything to do. Damned place was driving me mad.

From the dormitory to the front door was a long aisle. Each step Jean took she stamped. When she got to the door she shrieked to the nurse to let her out; her sobs were so loud I could hear them after the door had shut. When she returned she was jubilant. She came straight to me and produced a picture of a grey-haired woman. 'This is my adopted mummy.'

'I'm sorry, Jean, I never meant to be cruel. I get so bored.'

Jean told me I was here because I swore and behaved vulgarly, and when I learnt to be a lady I would go home.

'Yes, Jean, if you say so.'

Every night the lights went out at 8 p.m. The night staff came on duty at 10 p.m. and woke you up to give you sleeping-pills. I never took them. I could sleep without them.

'No thank you,' I would say.

'Refusing your pills?' Slap.

'No I'm not, I can sleep without them.'

'When did you become a doctor?' Slap.

One nurse held my mouth open while the other poured Largactil down my throat. What a carry-on. I didn't need sleeping-pills.

Mary was Irish and weighed 20 stone at least. When she walked she had to push her shoulders forward she was so huge.

Mary would grab my arm and make me listen to her life story. 'Now will you listen, when I was Queen of Denmark I had everything I wanted.'

'Queen of Denmark,' I would giggle.

Mary didn't slap me, she punched me. But I couldn't help laughing at her stories, although to her they were real life. She would punch me repeatedly on the upper arm until bruising appeared. Then another day she was a Harley Street doctor, so she would sit with my arm in a vice-like grip diagnosing everything from cancer to kidney failure — everything except that I needed her to stop punching me.

Another day she was the owner of the hospital. I said, 'Can I go home?'

'You go home, for the love of God, what do you think I am, a nutcase?'

My arm hurt too much already to say yes.

One day in the middle of the week Jean received a letter. As she was reading it she jumped up, screaming, and fell to the floor in a fit. Later it turned our her 'adopted mummy' had died. Jean was put to bed until the next morning.

Jean weighed 14 stone, and after this news she began to have regular fits. They were terrible to watch. She frothed and foamed at the mouth. She had a bad one at visiting time and was put into the PR for her own safety. She wouldn't eat or talk. She shouted to God to take her life so's to be with her 'adopted mummy'. They took away the ticking blankets and the jerry. Like Sylvia, Jean slept on the bare padding. She refused her food; sometimes they didn't bother to take her any.

My bed in the dormitory was closest to the pads. For three days and nights I didn't hear Jean screaming; I thought she was getting better. On the fourth day (I think it was a Sunday as I didn't go on the rounds), a couple of nurses put Jean in a wheelchair and pushed her back to her bed. Her head was slumped to one side and she looked an odd colour.

Mary grabbed my arm and dragged me to Jean's bed to be her assistant as she was a 'doctor' that day. Jean's head was still slumped in the same position, the blankets were up over her chest, and her arms were by her sides. I took her hands and said, 'Jean, I'm glad you're back, I've missed you.' I rubbed her hand; it was very cold. I presumed it was from lying on the bare padding.

Mary took her right arm and felt for her pulse. She then lifted Jean's eyelids. 'She's dead,' said Mary. Then she tucked her arms under the sheet and pulled the sheet over her face. 'She's dead,' she said, grabbing my arm and walking away.

I didn't believe Mary; she lived in a world of her own.

Later I was thinking how cold Jean had felt. I went along to Sister's office and told her what had happened and what Mary had said. 'Rubbish, you know what that loony's like. Humour her. Now get out.'

I went and thought no more of it.

Jean's face was still covered when the afternoon shift came on duty. A new nurse noticed this and went to investigate. I'm sure the first day on a locked ward is bad enough in itself for a young and inexperienced nurse, but to find a dead body as well was too much. The nurse screamed and fainted. From then on all hell was let loose. The staff were rushing around all over the place. Two tall men came and wheeled Jean's body out through the ward in a tin box.

I crawled under a chair and cried for Jean. 'Jean, may you rest in peace with your "adopted mummy".'

After so much suffering she never even got a decent funeral. No one to mourn her. No one to miss her. She is still vivid in my mind. She was a good kind woman, not to be forgotten.

After Jean had gone neither staff nor patients mentioned her again. It was like snuffing out a candle, or wiping away a piece of imaginary dirt.

I wonder why she called the lady her 'adopted mummy'. Never once did she call the lady just 'Mummy'.

6

SPEAKING OF LOVE

I need another Valium tablet. Damned pills depress me more than pep me. My mind feels like a juggling act, backwards and forwards, up and down. My head is so mixed up.

I just have to save my marriage. If it falls apart, where could I go except back to St Bernard's (where I belong and fit in)? Everyone who knows me will point their fingers and say, 'We told you so.' This isn't happening because I haven't tried. God knows I've tried.

I've lost a lot of weight.

For Sunday dinner I buy a three-and-a-half-pound chicken. Our week's shopping consists of chicken, two pounds of potatoes, a pound of cabbage, two pounds of sugar, a quarter of a pound of tea, a loaf of bread, six cheese spreads and little else. Sunday we have roast chicken, roast potatoes and cabbage. Monday we have the same but less. Tuesday the same but I don't have any. I have a cup of tea with six sugars so that I get the grams of carbohydrate I need.

Wednesday I go for a walk. Near here is a garden with one of the wood panels missing. I reach my hand in through the panel and take the vegetables off the lady's compost heap. I bring them home, cut up all the good bits of swede, turnip and potato (some days I even get a mushy tomato), put them into a saucepan with the last of the chicken and make a stew.

Thursday I go back to the compost for whatever is left. I put it into the saucepan on top of Wednesday's leftovers and there is another vegetable-cum-vegetable stew. Sheryl's food is liquidized so whatever I've got she gets.

Friday and Saturday I have my tea and sugar. Steve has his dinner at work and the stew when he comes home, but he needs it — after all, he is the breadwinner.

I'm going to bed. I've got to be up early to return the soldiers. I'm panicking. I'm frightened. I'm scared. Don't ask me what of because I don't know. My mouth tastes like a sack of nicotine. I feel as though I've been eating cigarettes, not smoking them. My stomach is turning over and over like a ball. Why am I so frightened?

Hold my hand. Dr Morrish, I wish you were here. You'd help me, wouldn't you? I loved you when I was there; I still love you. Please say you'll help me. I'm not well in my head, and I can't cope with being out here. I can't cope with not having enough money to feed my family. It means such a lot to know you'll help me. You will, won't you? I'm only 22. Help me see my way through to 23.

Mother, do you understand what I'm on about? I'm two weeks overdue on my period. I couldn't cope with another pregnancy now.

Susan you're a pathetic, self-centred, selfish bitch. You are totally worthless. Don't start crying, you're supposed to be a woman, not a little girl. You are not to cry. It's wrong.

I don't love my Steve any more. He made me love him with his gentle ways, but now he's made me dislike him. He has been good to me, too good in fact. He lets me rule the roost, dominate him, and leaves everything to me. He hasn't spoken to me for three weeks. I can't stand the deep piercing quiet; it unnerves me. I want him to check me when I have done something to annoy him; he won't though. I wish he were more of a man and didn't let me henpeck him. He won't acknowledge how I feel, even though I have tried to explain.

I want Sheryl to be reared in a good stable home. I know I can't make this for her. I'm mental and I don't love her daddy. I did once, but I don't know what has happened to the love I felt.

What the hell is love anyway? If I turn on the radio or watch the television there's that word 'love'. Love means emptiness and desolation to me.

I'm going to give Sheryl up for adoption to a couple who can give her all the things she needs. My heart is wrenching,

my eyes are crying, and my body aches with love for Sheryl.
But giving life isn't the end, is it? Someone reassure me.

I know I can't give her all the things she needs, like a good
environment, a strong mind and a mummy to love and
admire. I wish I could keep her as she is now, pure and
unknowing of all the ugly things in this lousy world.

I've failed my Sheryl. I've failed my Steve. I've failed my
mum. I'm useless. Mother, why did you give me life, enabling
me to give Sheryl life? Poor Sheryl. I love her so deeply. I must
give her up for her to have her life without inheriting my
mental disorders. I'm having a mental breakdown. Is there no
one who can help me?

My heart is breaking. I'm not worthy of anything. Parents
shouldn't tell their children that life is beautiful. Life is shit,
fucking downright shit. If I was dead I would be happy. I can't
keep pretending I'm all right. I'm not all right. I don't think I
was mental when I was 12, but now I'm 22 I'm truly mental.

I can't give Sheryl a good life of any kind if she stays with
me. Doesn't anyone out there understand? Steve doesn't.

The radio is on and someone is singing a song about Jesus at
6.45 a.m. How I wish I could believe in him.

Why is it when you're grown up people think you don't
need a strong arm to comfort you? If only Steve had the
capacity to put his arms around me. Will I ever come to terms
with my mentalness? Shut up, for God's sake. Why does my
life hurt so much? Can't anyone help me straighten myself
out? I'm not in command of my mind any more.

I feel good today. I must get myself into a routine. I will go
to bed early and rise early. Then I'll have more time. I will get
out in the fresh air every day with Sheryl.

Good girl, Susan, you must look to the future and be
grateful you are here at all.

I have a multitude of chores to do. Sheryl, you make my
heart swell. How beautiful you are. Chores, Susan, get off
your arse and get them done. I slept late again and I went to
bed early. Stupid bitch, can't even do a simple thing like get up
early.

Bruce is so friendly. He came to see Sheryl while she was sitting on the floor, and whipped her in the eye with his tail. I picked Sheryl up to give her a cuddle. She put her hand in my dinner, picked up a beefburger, slapped it in my face and gave it to Bruce.

It's Wednesday today and the fucking thoughts are back. Bastard pen's running out. I've found another one.

On Friday I wasn't well. On Saturday I smashed the clock. I was most upset when it still worked, so I smashed it on the floor until it was in bits. On Sunday I fell down the stairs. Sheryl's crying again. She's always complaining. No, that's a lie, she's a good baby; I hope to keep her that way. Steve doesn't make love to me any more.

Perhaps I ought to accept all these thoughts. After all, I did accept my adolescence in St Bernard's. I wish I could go back. I hate it out here. Steve is having trouble at work. He keeps going in late and they've told him unless he toes the line he'll have to go. Jobs are hard to find now. I must be to blame for his defiance. I'm too domineering. Stupid bastard lets me be domineering.

My sister Pam is getting married soon and moving to Germany. My younger sister, Pauline, is pregnant and getting married next week. I'm happy and a little bit sad too. I don't know why.

Damned potatoes are boiling. It's nearly Christmas. I look out of my window and the world is so barren — no warmth, no people, no children in the street shrieking with laughter as they do in the summer. I don't like the winter. Autumn and spring are the best times of year.

I'm still smoking like a trooper. It's a disgusting habit.

Things seem to be working out; how strange life is. I feel hopeful for the first time in ages.

7

LEARNING

I was 13, and a permanent resident on Ward 19. It was much more scary than the coal cellar.

I wanted to go back to school. I wanted to teach Sylvia more things. I kept begging them to let me go back to school. I must have put my case over well because they brought in a private tutor. Her name was Mrs Wharton. She was immaculate in her dress and tall, with steel-grey hair, thin lips and deep-set eyes. She made me feel inferior.

She seemed to me empty inside. She was wary of me because I was the nutcase. 'Good morning Susan. Sit down. Right, we'll start.'

At first I liked her. I had a feeling that she could help me get out of St Bernard's. I thought I'd be able to tell her how frightened I get, but she didn't want to know. She never once asked, 'How's Susan today?' She was cold, and I reacted badly once again.

I think she came for three weeks altogether. She taught me some French. Two songs I can still recite. One of them is about a duck on a pond who has lost her young and is searching frantically; the other is about a sad girl who has lost her way of life. At night when everyone was asleep I would softly croon the song about that young girl.

One day I went to Ellis Ward for my tuition, and began to tell Mrs Wharton about something that had happened the day before. She turned, without even letting me finish, and said, 'I have not the slightest interest or need to listen to anything you do in your time not spent here. Now sit and we'll start.'

I was so hurt by her indifference. 'Damn right we'll fucking start, you old slag.' I was shaking with anger.

41

There wasn't a nurse present and Mrs Wharton was fumbling with the door handle. All the staff had heard what I'd called her, and Sister Selby was pushing me up against the wall talking about leopards not changing their spots. I flung my arms in the air and shouted, 'Fuck off, the lot of you.' I fled Ellis and went back to 19s on my own.

In three weeks I'd gained 15 hours' tutoring, two weeks' punishment for my outburst, and an understanding that people didn't care whether I was 13 or 30, in a mental home on a locked ward or not. I tried to get back on the rounds, but Sister wouldn't let me because old Minnie who counted the cutlery had started doing it since I'd been going to school. I was not going to do the polishing and waxing again; I'd do anything but that.

I was allowed, with a nurse, to make the beds in wards 12 and 13. These were geriatric wards and I was told to help — to bedbath them, feed the ones who couldn't feed themselves, and change and make their beds. The first time I went my stomach heaved. The smell of the old was dreadful. I had never seen such filth. Most of the old ladies were lying in their own mess. Some were smearing it all over themselves and their cots, some were eating it.

I worked seven days a week, 9 a.m. to 12 noon and 1.30 to 4 p.m. One day a nurse told me I was to clean up the old ladies instead of making beds. I said I would. There was one old lady called Pussy (because she stroked her fanny). Pussy was 83 years old and really sweet, except she was always covered in shit. She was heavy and could only be bedbathed. I never saw her out of bed once in the 18 months I worked there. After she was washed she was turned over on her side, and at the base of her spine were ulcers. At first they were only running, but then they started bleeding. The nurse washed her back, threw some talc over it, then rubbed in surgical spirit. Pussy effed and blinded, stroking her fanny.

Between wards 12 and 13 there were 180 beds, all occupied by old infirm ladies. There were so many ladies like Pussy that they only got their ulcers tended every four days. By the time each lady's turn came round they were in an awful state. I prayed that if I was still in St Bernard's when I became old (at that time there was no reason to believe I wouldn't be) I would be spared such suffering and indignity. I tried to tend Pussy's ulcers every day. I wished I could do them all but I couldn't. I found myself biting back the anger I felt for the suffering of these old folk and most days reacting badly yet again by being disgustingly rude to everyone.

Funny though it may seem, I enjoyed cleaning the old ladies and tending their ulcers. I felt I was being useful — and I'm a terrific bed-maker even now.

I didn't like it when the staff were busy and got bad tempered; they were rough with the old ladies. Sometimes the nurses rubbed the old ladies' noses in their own shit. I will never forget when three nurses were having some fun with two of the old ladies. After rubbing them in shit, they tipped their Complan over their heads and left them like that until nearly 3 p.m. About 2.30 p.m. I got upset and shouted at them to clean them up or else let me clean them. They laughed at me. I screamed, 'You're the fucking nutters,' and went to the sluice room to get a bowl of water to wash the ladies. The nurses followed me and grabbing me by the hair dragged me along to the shitty women. They rubbed my face in Grace's face which was covered in shit. She was spitting and dribbling. For weeks after I smelt of shit.

I was 12½ and had been in 19s about five months when I thought I might have a bath. Once a week everyone would strip off their clothes by their beds and trail into the bathroom. There they were handed a towel, which had already been used by three other patients. About 98 per cent of the patients were over 16 stone, and the sight of them standing naked for sometimes two hours was funny.

It was on this occasion that I witnessed two of the women having sex. Pauline and Bernadette. Pauline was tall and thin with close-cropped hair; her eyes were close together, her nose was long and she didn't have any lips. From behind she looked like a man. Bernadette was not quite as tall as Pauline, but equally thin; she had short curly hair and she never stopped giggling. Pauline initiated the sex by licking between Bernadette's legs. Bernadette was writhing around like someone possessed. Then she did the same to Pauline. They were both standing and never got out of line or missed their place in the queue. At first I looked away, but everyone else was looking and some even followed their lead.

When it was my turn, I went into the bathroom (there were two nurses with the bath keys supervising), sheepishly took off my clothes and pulled the plug out. Fifty-eight patients had been in that bath water without it being changed once. The scum was thick and the smell of underarm and vaginal sweat was vile. The nurses pushed my head under the water, shouting, 'Susan Read, you're a fucking upstart. Who do you think you are to have fresh water?'

How did I know? I thought the idea of having a bath was to get clean, not to become dirtier. After that incident I never set foot in the bathroom for the duration of my stay in 19s, three and a half years.

When I went to Hammersmith Hospital for my diabetic check-up, Dr Lowie gave me an examination. About eight months had elapsed since the bathroom incident, so I wasn't too rosy. Dr Lowie was horrified when she started examining me. 'Judging by the state and smell of you, you can't have washed in six months. I could grow potatoes in your neck. Your mother is a fine upstanding woman. You should be disgusted with yourself. You deserve to be where you are, at least until you can behave like a reasonable human being.'

If you had known, Dr Lowie, how I did live. It was hardly at all like a human being.

I felt ashamed after what Dr Lowie had said, so when I got back to 19s I thought, if I can't have a bath I can at least wash. In the room before you reached the bathroom there were four sinks along the wall on each side, with a mirror over each sink. I went into the wash-basin room and pulled a portable screen around myself. I undressed except for my knickers. I washed my face and neck. It was difficult to see if they were clean because the mirror over the sink was shattered. I washed under my arms and dried myself; then I removed my knickers to wash my private parts. I was drying myself when Pauline came in and really hurt me. If she had been a man it would have been called rape, but she wasn't, so I don't know what it was called. She bit my bosoms and roughly pushed her fingers and mouth between my legs. I cried and screamed, 'Help!'

Benson heard the noise and came into the washroom. I was pinned to the floor. Benson kicked the side of my head and threatened, 'Wrap up cunt, you'll get the PR.' She stood and watched that bitch do those things to me.

When it was over they left the room and I lay there on the cold tiled floor for a long time. I was bleeding down below and I was dirty again after struggling on the dirty floor. But my body was dirtier inside, and no amount of bathing would ever wash that away.

After that I got worse. In fact I got mental.

I wasn't sure how to smoke; I'd drag on the cigarette gently and blow out noisily without inhaling. Sylvia taught me how to smoke her way: she swallowed the smoke. I choked and made my throat sore for days.

Sister Hutchins was old — about 50ish — and walked as though she was going to take off at any moment. When she came on duty she would sweep through the length of the ward, shouting and bawling at people about different things. 'Sleeping is forbidden in my ward. Get up, Read ... Picking your nose again, Doreen ... Doris, stop that snivelling.' It never ceased to amaze me how she could sweep through the ward so fast without missing anything and with us patients not seeing her. I called her Gran Hutchins behind her back because she looked so old, and she knew.

When we queued for our pills, if I asked for an aspirin because I had a headache, the nurse would say loudly, 'Have you got your period?' followed by roughly squeezing my bosoms. Everything was loud and everyone knew. 'Had your shit today?' everyone would laugh.

The first time she (they all did it) squeezed my bosoms, I knocked her hand to one side and said 'Piss off'. Three nurses decided I had assaulted her, and grabbing me by the scruff of my neck they spun me round from one to the other. As I reached each one they either slapped my face or pulled my hair, squeezed my bosoms or kicked my shins. They did this continually for about an hour and a half. I didn't like having bosoms.

I hated the daytime, but night-time was even worse. Nurse never paid any attention to who did what all night. The bad patients were double-locked in their rooms. Nurse would sit in the office. Pauline would climb into my bed and roughly fuck me. She was strong and I was so scared.

After I was raped I'd made friends with a girl called Linda. She was very violent with people for no reason. One night I was lying wide awake, dreading the nightly assault by Pauline; my heart was pounding. I leapt out of my bed and sneaked in beside Linda. She was asleep and I made her jump. She slapped me sharply across my face. I didn't cry. I never cried any more; to cry was a weakness. I carefully made to move out of her bed. I thought she was going to attack me the way I'd seen her attack others on her bad days. Instead she pulled me back into her bed and cuddled me. I fell asleep with my head nestled into Linda's shoulder. I awoke that night to find Linda stroking my bosoms. Very softly she was saying, 'Poor little tits.'

I wasn't worried. I fell back to sleep.

My sister Pam would bring me tights, scents, soaps and pretty bikini briefs when she visited. I'd started smoking quite early on, and was smoking 40 a day when I could get them. I soon learnt that nice things bought cigarettes. I would swap a pair of tights or pretty briefs for one cigarette. Sometimes Pam would bring me a number of things, and as soon as she had gone I would swap the lot. I never thought about later on; I could only think about that minute.

If a visitor put out a dog-end, I was amongst the ones who pounced for the shavings. As many as six women would fight for one dog-end. In the beginning I would come off quite badly; then I closed my mind and behaved like them. After a while I nearly always got the filthy dog-end. I learnt to open them and empty the shavings. Most times I would roll a makeshift fag with newspaper or toilet paper or I would intimidate another patient for fag papers. When I was lucky and got a long dog-end I'd put it in my mouth and beg someone for a light. We weren't allowed matches. Some visitors would bring me in 10 fags. Gran Hutchins went spare if she caught me smoking.

I began to shuffle like all the others. The whole ward shuffled except Gran Hutchins, and she swept everywhere. My shoulders were stooped, my feet shuffled and I was an animal. I lay in bed one night and wondered why I shuffled. I'd tried hard to straighten myself up but I couldn't. I'd noticed that everyone walked with this stooped shuffle. I tried to be like them so that I fitted in better. Whenever I stated that I wasn't mad or behaved in my kind of 'normal' way, I was subjected to jeers and asked questions I couldn't answer or just pushed backwards and forwards between two nurses amidst shrieks of laughter. So I decided to become outwardly like the other inmates, which would enable me to mingle without being noticed too often.

But after a while it went wrong, and I couldn't separate myself from them.

More and more I would sneak into Linda's bed, because Pauline's attacks were becoming more frequent. Linda never interfered with me; she gently stroked and kissed me.

Once when Sylvia was out of the pads I sneaked into her bed and tried to do to her what Linda did to me. I ran my hands over her nippleless bosoms and down over her savagely scarred tummy towards her vagina. I did this because I wanted Sylvia to know I cared for her. I only ran my hands over her the once, and she woke up. She clenched her fist and cuffed me on the side of my head. Dazed, I went back to my bed and felt very lonely. I hated the world for isolating me. To this day, with that scene still fresh in my mind, I can only say that Sylvia not only didn't feel pain, but also didn't feel joy.

8

DAPHNE AND FLORRIE

I was sleeping curled up in a chair. Gran Hutchins swept through the ward, yelling, 'Read, sleeping is forbidden on my ward. How long have you been here? Get up. Get up.'

I leapt out of the chair and at that moment saw someone drop a dog-end. I pounced and got it. It was still alight; I dragged deeply. Then I saw him and I loved him straight away. I still love him to this day. He was tall, though slightly round-shouldered, with a mass of black hair, a moustache and beard, and eyes that smiled life back into me. I dropped the fag on the floor and shuffled up behind this beautiful man. I fell in love with him like a woman does.

Sister Dickinson was the other duty Sister. Dickinson was tall and blonde, well groomed and sometimes very kind. She didn't sweep along like Gran; she stomped, dragging her right leg. It was more noticeable when she was tired. She didn't shout. She spoke precisely and deliberately. Not many people could pretend not to understand her.

Dickinson took the man into the office. I was crestfallen. He hadn't even noticed me.

Later I was called into the office. The first question he asked me was, 'How old are you, Sue? I can call you Sue, can't I?'

I felt compromised. I told him my age. 'You new here?'
He nodded.

'Listen mate, you don't ask people things here, you tell them.'
I sat silently. He smiled warmly and patted his knee. I turned my nose up and raised my eyes to the ceiling as if to imply he was nutty. He patted his knee again. 'Would you like to sit on my lap, Sue?'

'Are you a doctor?'

'Yes. Dr Morrish.'

'And you want *me* to sit on your lap?'

'Yes, Sue, if you'd like to.'

I was confused. He didn't tell me, he asked me. I didn't sit on his lap, because I smelt and I didn't want him to know. I hadn't washed in a long time.

'Would you like me to come next week, Sue?'

'If you want, I don't care,' I lied, praying he would.

The day before he was due I covered myself in deodorant perfume and dry shampoo. My hair was long and greasy. Linda clipped it behind my ears and lent me two pink ribbons.

When he walked in, my heart was pounding so loud I was sure everyone could hear it. Since he'd left I'd eaten, drank and slept him. He was the most beautiful man I'd ever encountered in my life. Sylvia said, 'He's here, Jenny, your visitor's here.'

'I'm not bothered. If he wants me he can come and get me,' I said, pretending to be indifferent.

As before, he went with Sister to her office. She called me. 'Read, you're wanted.'

I sat not moving. If he wanted me to sit on his lap last time, he would surely come and find me.

'Read, get here now.'

'Fucking bitch,' I muttered. I got my ear clipped as I shuffled past her. 'Fucking bitch,' I said again so that only my ears heard it.

Dr Morrish was standing when I went into the office. 'Sit down please, Sue.' He motioned towards the chair next to the desk.

'No.' I went over and looked out of the window.

'What can you see, Sue?'

'Nothing.'

'Why not?'

'I don't fucking know. What do you want me to see?'

Christ, he was so kind. I wanted to cry but I'd given up on crying. He had my case notes in front of him. 'Do you miss your daddy, Sue?'

'Do I fuck.'

'Do you fuck?'

I was speechless for a moment. Then I said, 'Mind your own fucking business.'

'Did you say you were 13½?'

I nodded.

'Are you going to stay here for ever, or do you want to leave?'

'Leave here and go where, who's going to have me? You've got a lot to learn mate, didn't they tell you what a hopeless case I am?' I was always shouting or talking loud since there was always such a rumpus going on. Even when there was silence I talked loud. I could hear my voice bounce back in my head and would try to moderate it without success.

'Do you think you're mad, Sue?'

'What? You're the bleeding doctor; you tell me.'

'No, let's hear what you think of yourself. Do you think you're mad?'

'Of course I'm mad. They all reckon so, and who'm I to argue? I'm outnumbered.'

He nodded and made sympathetic noises.

'When I behave nicely it's not worth it, I only get laughed at. So I'll be safe and mad thanks.'

We sat in silence for a while. 'Sue, I want to help you.'

'Yes? Open them locked doors and say that.'

'I can't do that, not until you've proved you're capable of being a little more grown up.' The doctor made a face as though he wanted to bite back those words.

'You stupid git, I'm only a kid. How can I behave grown up?' I slammed out of the office. Dickinson passed me and I shouted at her, 'Fucking old bitch.'

Slap. 'Read, go quieten down somewhere.' Benson came running up. 'It's OK, Benson, I've seen to Read.'

Benson looked deprived. I looked her square in the eyes and said, 'Cunt.'

Dickinson slapped me again and I shuffled off. 'Leave it, Benson,' Dickinson said, meaning it.

I parked myself in a chair after grabbing Doreen's dog-end.

I smoked the fag noisily and tried to make my mind a blank. I knew I wouldn't see him again. Just for a second I wondered why I never let anyone help me. 'Who cares? I don't need their fucking help. I'm past it.'

Mum came on Tuesdays. She talked to the ward Sister for ages. I hated it. Sometimes she would take me out in the grounds, depending on the kind of advice she had from Sister. We went out for a walk one Tuesday and Mum said, 'Sister said if I write out a pass for the weekend and you promise to be good you can come home on Friday.'

'I will be good, I promise.'

'All right Shue.'

'Great.' I ran off down the path.

'Shue, Shue, I won't do the pass unless you stay with me.'

'Fuck it,' I said in my head, and went back to link arms with Mum. 'Let's walk like soldiers, Mum.' If one of us skipped when we were walking, we went back into step.

The pass was put in writing, asking if I could spend a weekend with my family. It was signed by my mother. Mum said she would pick me up on Friday evening and I must promise to be good. I duly promised. Friday came. I'd had my things packed since Mum had left on Tuesday. I kissed Linda and Sylvia, saying I was going home. 'For good?' they said in unison.

'No, only for the weekend. I'll see you Sunday night.'

A whole weekend at home — I couldn't believe it. I thought about what I was going to do. Mostly I would go to the park. I would swing all day. I was going home and my mind was full of pretending. I would be 'normal' for two days. I would be so good, too, I said to myself over and over.

It was evening when we got home. I had my insulin and Mum cooked a delicious dinner. She was good to me. She let me stay up and watch the television until 10.30 p.m. I went to my own bed that night and slept like a log.

When I awoke the following morning I couldn't remember feeling happier. Mum and I went to Long Drive shops and I helped her carry the shopping home. It was about 11 a.m. by this time. After a cup of tea and a couple of biscuits, I got up to go out. 'See you later.'

'Where are you going, Shue?'

'To the park,' I said, irritated.

'Now sit down, Shue, you know I can't let you go to the park.'

'But why, Mum? I haven't been to the park for years.'

'Now Shue, you promised you'd be good, you did. I can't let you go off on your own to the park, or anywhere else for that matter.'

I was cross by this time. I couldn't figure out how wanting to go to the park for a swing was bad, and I felt threatened by being reminded that I'd promised to be good when I *was* being good. 'I'm going to the park.'

She stood in front of me, saying, 'No you're not, I'll get Mr Chilton if you try.' Mr Chilton was our next-door neighbour.

'Well go and fucking get him,' I shouted, running up the street in the direction of the park.

I had been at the park for 10 minutes when Mum and Mr Chilton turned up. 'Now come on home, Shue, you've been to the park, you have, you promised you'd be good.'

There were lots of kids around I'd known in the Juniors. 'Leave me alone, I want to stay here.'

'Mr Chilton, if I pay you for the petrol would you take Susan back now, as she doesn't seem able to behave herself?'

'Fuck off, fuck off and leave me alone.'

All the kids moved away. I mimicked a gorilla and tickled my lips. Then I ran off towards home. I sat in the kitchen and ate a pound of apples and a packet of custard creams before they got back. Thereafter I did everything noisily. I filled the kettle, half drowning the kitchen, and slammed it down on the gas stove.

Mum came in with her face set. 'Shue, you're a silly girl to yourself. I really thought we were going to have a nice weekend, and all you've done is upset everyone, including poor Mr Chilton.'

'Fuck off, cunt,' I spat at her.

I was taken back to 19s for being wicked and uncontrollable. Mum knocked on the main door. Gran Hutchins was on duty. Mum left me at the door and went into the office. I stomped off and put my things back in my locker. When Mum came out of the office she said, 'Goodbye Susan. Be good.'

I watched her walk to the main door with Sister and talk some more. Thud, followed by the clattering of keys. Gran swept along the ward. 'Read, my office now.'

'Shit, here we go again,' I said in my head. I knocked on the door.

'Come in.'

I went in.

'The first time you go home in a long time and what do you do?'

I flung myself into the chair by her desk. 'I only went to the park. Since when's that been a crime?'

Gran bodily tipped me out of the chair, shrieking that my mum was a fine woman doing her best for me and all I ever did was cause her trouble. 'You're not the only one she's got to think of, you know.'

'Christ almighty, I only went to the park and everyone goes stupid.'

'Manners, Read, you use manners when you're talking to me.' I stood and let her shout and holler what a wicked and indescribable person I was. 'Believe you me, Read, if I've got anything to do with it, it will be a long time before you go home again.'

I discovered that when I behaved like all the other patients the pressure wasn't as tight as usual. I forced myself to chain smoke. I learnt how to roll used dog-ends in loo paper. I wanted to fit in and not be under a constant light. The nurses shrieked with laughter and singled me out for rough treatment whenever I said, 'I'm not mad, I'm all right, honest I am.' Once they stripped me off and plunged me into a bath of cold water someone had excreted in. They washed me with this piece of shit, dragged me out and dressed me in a bit of cotton material with no buttons and a pair of check slippers with bobbles. Every time I yelled they tipped a bucket of water over my head and I had the sensation of drowning.

After this I decided that to these 'normal' people I would

have to appear mental. On the rare occasions I was alone I would collect all my normal thoughts and make-believe I was living somewhere else. After a while I started to forget what 'normal' was. I don't think I decided at any given time that I was either normal or abnormal; things just seemed to catch up on me.

Daphne was a slim, attractive woman of 35ish. She spoke nicely and it was said that she was a schoolteacher. She was quiet and spoke only when she was asked a question. All the staff and patients picked on Daphne, so I took care of her. Everywhere Daphne was, I was too.

I'm ashamed to say it all got a bit out of hand. At the first opportunity I got away from a cruel situation.

Smash. Smash. Daphne's head would rock from side to side. They didn't slap her head, they punched it. 'Open your fucking mouth,' Benson would say.

Daphne would sit, her body perfectly straight and still, lips set in a stiff line. Daphne wouldn't eat no matter what they did to her. I liked Daphne and got angry when she let them beat her up. All she had to do was eat. I'd try to get her to eat, saying, 'For Christ's sake Daph, eat, will you, then they'll leave you alone.'

Smash — straight across my mouth. 'Mind your fucking business, Read,' Benson yelled. she turned her attention to me. 'Come on, you eat it.' Every time they'd tried to put something into Daphne's mouth she had dribbled it back on to her plate. They swapped my plate for Daphne's and forced me to eat it. I did, eventually. My arms and chin were bruised. Now, all these years later, my stomach retches as I recall that episode.

The following day, with what little bit of sanity I had left, I decided that unless I wanted that to happen each meal time I should move to another table. When they knocked Daphne about I couldn't ignore it. I never could keep my mouth shut even for my own good. Even to this day I can't let injustices go without saying my piece. They wouldn't let me move. Each day was a nightmare. They played on my wanting to move and beat Daphne worse. Bastards. I never saw Daphne eat a morsel of food while she was an inmate on 19s.

One morning I got into a fight with Susan, which ended with Sylvia going back to the pads. I shuffled around, looking for Daphne. I couldn't find her anywhere. When I asked the nurses where she was, they said, 'Who's Daphne?'

I know Daphne was in her bed when I went to sleep that night, yet when I woke up next morning her bed was made up new. I searched the ward but still there was no sign of Daphne. The bastards told me I was going mental and they'd never heard of anyone called Daphne. At pill times and meal times they'd shout out, 'Daphne, you're late again. Where are you, woman? Read, have you seen her?'

I despised them for their cruelty.

Florrie was deliriously happy. She crouched over, taking long strides, and bobbed up and down when she walked. Her face was long and thin, with a hooked nose and twinkly eyes. She wasn't violent, but if you didn't know her she could be unnerving. She would make towards you very fast and stop just in front of you, place her face square in front of yours and laugh hysterically.

When Florrie had her period she behaved strangely — so strangely that she was locked in a side-room until her period had finished. She'd undress (she was pitifully thin) and mess everywhere. She played games with it, smearing it all over the walls, shampooed her hair and ate it. She wouldn't wear a sanitary towel. She'd squat on the floor, bearing down, and when she lost blood she would let it flow into her hands and drink it. She'd lie on the cold floor of her room, cackling, and masturbate with a spoon-handle.

Florrie was forever losing her false teeth. They turned up in the most peculiar places. One time they were lost for six months. She looked so funny without them; her face became shrunken and caved in. One day there were sausages and plum tomatoes for breakfast. There, stuck in a sausage, were Florrie's teeth. Everyone laughed, even sour old Benson. The staff were never unkind to Florrie. When her period had finished she was all right.

Florrie's mum (she came every Thursday) died. Nobody told Florrie. In her handbag she had old letters from her mum, saying she would be coming to see her on Thursday. On a day when she was without her period she showed me an old letter saying her mum was coming. When her mum didn't arrive, Florrie insisted that something must be wrong. She tried to take the keys from the nurse to go and search for her mum. The nurses grabbed her and bundled her into the side-room. They told her her mum was dead. Florrie was never all right again. She spent her days in the side-room masturbating and playing with her excrement amidst shrieks of laughter.

Florrie was still there when I left St Bernard's at 17.

9

MOVING

I was 14 when Ward 19 was moved next door into Ward 18. Every patient, every stick of furniture, everything — including me — was moved. At this time my existence was very bad. Dr Morrish did come back and was around quite often in the early days of Ward 18.

Wards 18 and 19 were opposite each other with the stairs in between. As you walked through the door of Ward 18, to the left was the kitchen, quite large in comparison to 19's kitchen. On the right were two side-rooms which immediately became Nellie's and Gladys's. Further up was the linen room. Straight ahead, slightly to the right, were 16 tables seating four at each. To the left past the tables was the sitting area, with a television and about 30 chairs. Off the sitting area was a long corridor which consisted of double-locked rooms, six on each side. My mind would venture down that corridor. Only my mind; for some reason I couldn't physically go down there. As I sit here now my body fills with a terror so great I'm shaking.

Back in the sitting area to the left was the dormitory, with at least 70 beds. The dormitory was partitioned off by little glass windows and a glass-panelled door. Behind the partition were five rooms which were not locked and a toilet with a sink. The smell in the toilet was as odious as in 19's dormitory toilet. Along from the dormitory were three windows with three chairs underneath. Up a short ramp was the main door, which was used more than the other one. Along the ramp was a wooden railing with three more chairs. Opposite the railing were the toilets and bathroom area. To the left of the main door were two more double-locked rooms and two offices. One was Sister's office and the other was the medicine room.

There were a number of patients left on Ward 18 when we moved in. I didn't like this change around; it unsettled everyone. From the time we moved until the time I left about 18 months later, not a day passed without someone smashing out the windows or fighting. It was horrible, violent mayhem.

I was still helping out on wards 12 and 13. In the mornings I went on the rounds. It could have been because I hadn't been on the rounds for so long, but it seemed different, even though we still went to the same places. There was a fellow who worked in the kitchen area who paid me a great deal of attention. He'd wolf-whistle and say, 'Yoo-hoo sexy Sue.' He'd wink at me and pucker up his lips making kissing noises. I thought it was great to be fancied and I'd give him a flash of my knickers. He'd whoop with delight.

The nurse had a boyfriend in the kitchen area and would disappear for 15 to 20 minutes. It was a hot day and I was wearing a white and blue spotted summer dress with thin shoulder-straps. I was sitting at the end of the barrow, fanning myself with an envelope.

'Sue, do you want 10 bob?'

I spun round and saw the fellow who called me sexy Sue. I stood up and wiggled my hips. 'Oh yes, what for?'

'Give us a quick feel, go on, 10 bob.'

'You aren't touching me mate, piss off you dirty git.'

'No Sue, *you* give me a feel.' He showed me a 10-shilling note.

I snatched it from him, shoving it in my slippers. He grabbed me, leading me behind some metal dinner trolleys. He withdrew his penis and, taking my hand, placed it around the end. I closed my eyes and rubbed twice; he immediately ejaculated over my hand. I snatched my hand away, and wiping it on the arm of his overall I ran back to the barrow.

'Where you been, Read?' the nurse said, slapping me round the ear.

'Get off.' I pushed the barrow back the way we'd come. That was my first experience with a man. My hand was sticky. I kept pressing it on the barrow-handle and pulling it away.

That afternoon I went to help on the geriatric wards. At the end of Ward 13 was a double door. To the right was a flight of stairs. Straight ahead was the patients' canteen. The canteen was old and filthy. The floor was wood boards that had years of crusted dog-ends, spilt tea and coffee, phlegm and semen encrusted into it. There were men and women sitting around who'd been there for 30 years or more. A man and a woman sat in the far corner, loudly arguing. They snorted and spat green mucus on the floor. Men masturbated their limp penises, and everyone fought for dog-ends. I had 10 bob that day and bought 10 Park Drive. I asked someone for a light and she made a grab for my fag. I punched her above the ear and she backed off, cursing. I'd learnt long ago that I must never back down or I'd be trodden on.

Anne left an impression on me that still makes me break out in a cold sweat. She was a Scots woman who was a long-term patient. She was 46 years old, five feet tall and sharp-featured, with long, jet-black hair. She would get highs and lows. Her highs she spent talking about her son, who according to her was the reason she was in there. She'd laugh a hoarse, guttural laugh and say, 'Anne fucked once. Anne got caught. Anne had a darling baby boy. That's why Anne's here. Anne's not mad, Anne got fucked.'

I believed her. She probably wasn't mad when she went in there, but she was definitely mad when I knew her. The story was that Anne had had her son illegitimately.

When Anne got her low period she scared the hell out of me. She would pace the same three feet of floor. She mumbled incoherently the whole time. In the morning she would go berserk and create havoc. She'd start at breakfast by turning the tables over, regardless of who was there. Needless to say, you were lucky if you weren't scalded or covered in food. I never sat at Anne's table or anywhere near it. After she'd turned over the tables she would stand with her legs apart, her hands on her hips, and scream in a Scots accent, 'Come on, you Irish fucker, try your luck with me.'

I'd hide under a chair. Once Anne started, the whole ward followed. There would be pandemonium. Everyone would punch out the windows, smash the crockery and throw the tables and chairs. Anne was vicious. Not a nurse, Gran Hutchins nor Dickinson would approach her. They had a bell they used to summon help. It always took at least six nurses to overpower her. Anne would go stiff and she looked as though she was unconscious. They'd inject her with paraldehyde and throw her in the pads.

Nellie was Irish and weighed about 26 stone. She was a privileged patient, even though she rarely left the ward. Rumour had it that Nellie had murdered her husband, her parents and two children with an axe. As Nellie was so large, whenever there was a disturbance Nellie was allowed to wade in and stop it however she saw fit. The only one Nellie couldn't beat was Anne. As small as Anne was, Nellie always looked a pitiful sight after Anne had encouraged her to 'come on and get' her. Nellie never learnt to leave Anne alone. Nellie maintained that one day she would get the 'Scotch bastard'. She never did while I was there.

Cynthia was five feet 11 inches tall and scraggily thin. She had huge brown eyes that were sunken in their sockets, a button nose and a full-lipped mouth. Her hands and feet both turned out. She was an artist and drew the loveliest pictures. Her father visited her every week. He would leave £20 with her on each visit and say, 'Darling, if Daddy can help in any way, don't hesitate what.'

Cynthia showed interest in everything I said and did. If I said, 'Fuck it,' Cynthia would say, 'No, Susan Fish, say fish not mmmm.'

Cynthia was like Sylvia in the way she treated herself, but she only slashed her wrists.

Elizabeth was 20 and would cause havoc at visiting time. She was a pretty girl, with brown Afro-style hair. She was feminine in the extreme and wore thick make-up. There weren't many visitors for the long-term patients. A visitor would sit down and place her handbag at her feet. Elizabeth would stroll over, pick up the bag and walk away. You could see the wheels turning as the visitor looked around for a nurse. There was never a nurse when you needed one. The visitor would decide to tackle the situation herself.

'Excuse me dear, you seem to have picked up my handbag. Could I have it back please?'

'Mine, my bag,' Elizabeth would shout, clutching the bag to her chest.

The frantic visitor would try again. 'No dear, it's my bag.'

Elizabeth would turn the bag out, relating different stories to each article. 'See, it is mine,' she would yell, sobbing as she walked away.

Sister would intervene at some stage, but not before the poor visitor was a nervous wreck. My mum and Pam always had their bags taken by Elizabeth. Liz really believed they were hers.

Caroline was 19 years old and had four children. Each one was conceived by another inmate, called Mac, who was 79 years old. Each time she had one of his children he gave her £100. Caroline's uncle used to visit Mac, and she went along too. She had two children by him before anyone realized he was the father. She didn't seem mentally ill to me, although her mentality was childlike. After she became an inmate in St Bernard's she had two more children by Mac. Many times this disgusting old man propositioned me — to no avail. They took her babies away. Caroline didn't mind.

Myra slept in the bed next to mine. She rolled herself to sleep. I tried it but it made me sick.

Sarah was a 22-year-old half-caste. She had an obsession that if anyone or anything touched her she would become pregnant. She washed herself continually. She created many disturbances day and night with her obsession.

I was rotting inside my head. My mind was absorbing all the violence and degradation. I wrote a letter to Dr Blair, asking if I could go back to school. Swakeleys was an all-girls school, so this is where I was sent. Prevention is better than cure was their motto.

Mrs Bennett picked me up at Ward 18 and brought me back each day. I liked cooking. Mrs George, the cookery teacher, was kind to me. Lunchtime was awful. As they had at the previous school, they put me at a table by myself. I hated it. Everything got dramatized. I felt they were singling me out.

I had been there nearly two months when the headmistress called me into her office and told me off. I can't remember what for. I ran out of the office, out of the school and over the main road to Mrs Bennett's house. After that the headmistress said either I was removed or she resigned. The authorities never let me go to school again. They said I was my own worst enemy. No doubt they were right.

Gran Hutchins gave me a birthday tea and lace-embroidered handkerchiefs for each of my birthdays. To this day I have those five sets of hankies.

Kath and Rosina were the best of friends and had been in St Bernard's for as long as they could remember. They were as alike as shit and sugar. Kath was reasonably clever and quite posh, while Rosina was a cockney and a bit thick. Rosina agreed with everything Kath said, whether it was right or wrong.

Sheila worked outside, at a jeweller's. She was rather fat; her ankles hung over the edges of her shoes. My mum bought me a watch and the strap broke. Sheila bought me a bracelet-type strap and asked nothing for it.

To perfect my handwriting I'd copy things out of books or write swear words over and over. I'd get so cross in the end that my writing became illegible. Pauline would come along and, leaning over me, rub my bosoms. Benson would shout, 'If you two have to do that, do it elsewhere.'

'Get her off me.'

Pauline would drag me into the loos. The smell of sex in there was rampant. I learnt not to say anything to dissuade her, because she would only get me later. I'd sit or lie down, however she put me. As long as I didn't protest she was usually satisfied with a half-hour. I had to close my eyes and let my mind wander away to enable me to get through those wretched minutes, which became more and more regular as I was growing up.

This butch Pauline repulsed me. I hated her with every fibre in my body; what she did to me was torture. But I loved Linda. I'd climb into her bed when she wasn't in the PR and snuggle up to her. She cuddled me and stroked my bosoms. I felt so close to her and I didn't mind her affection and physical love for me. Yes, she loved me and I loved her and I needed her gently to touch me. I couldn't be all that bad if just one person in amongst all this shit could love me for myself and ask nothing in return.

10

FAILING

Even when I'm busy my head is thinking.

I can't understand how Steve can sit and not speak at all. It's three months since Steve has spoken a word to me. He doesn't bath or wash his hair. Five and a half months have gone by since we made love. Not that I want to, with him smelling like a skunk. Damned bastard man, he drives me mad with his dirty habits and silence.

I went out Friday night for a laugh with a crowd of girls I knew when I worked at the hospital. Yesterday my friend Linda was here; I gave her a detailed version of Friday night, except I said I'd spent it with a man. When she was about to go, I said to Steve, in front of her, 'Do you remember when you said if ever I was unfaithful to you you'd divorce me?'

Steve nodded, grunting.

'Well you'd better see a solicitor, because last night I was.'

Silence. Linda put on her coat. She did not approve; she called me a bitch with her eyes. Steve took Linda home. When he got back he broke his silence. 'Who was it? I want to know, you dirty cow. Just because I haven't been in the mood doesn't mean you can go with the first bloke who comes along. You obviously didn't give Sheryl or me a thought, did you?' He glared at me and walked towards the door, saying, 'Look at all those months you were in hospital having Sheryl, and I never even thought of doing anything like that.'

'Don't go blaming me for your abnormalities,' I spat at him. I had been in hospital nearly six months when I was pregnant with Sheryl, and he denied even having a wank. Either I'm a nymphomaniac or he just isn't sexually turn-on-able.

He told me I was a dirty old bag and disappeared upstairs.

64

When he came down it was apparent he'd bathed and washed his hair. He sat beside me and cuddled me on to his lap.

The truth is I wanted a reaction from Steve. I wanted to see if he cared. For the first time in our marriage Steve and I changed roles. He did all the talking and accusing. That was what I wanted, so I played the highest card — and won.

I know I'm not perfect, but surely Steve must feel something for me. I can't be that sexless and unlovable, can I? He says yes. Yes I'm totally unlovable. I'm still in an uneasy het-up state. It's ages since I've felt hopeful. I know the answer to this isn't simple, but Steve has to be involved; I can't sort it out on my own. Giving up work was a mistake. Steve and I aren't any closer, and as for talking, we've drawn a big zero.

Steve doesn't talk. I think he's lost his voice. We don't have a television, so it's not as if he sits and watches that. No, he just sits and stares. I try to get close to him, to be warm and kind, but he's like a dead man. Even when we're in bed, if I turn over and snuggle up for a cuddle or because I'm cold, he moves me away. I don't exist. I feel so unwanted. Whatever did I do to deserve this rejection all through my life? I'm sure that physically Steve can't make love any more. I've tried taking the initiative, but he won't let me. He won't even let me cuddle him. I've asked Steve what is bothering him; I wish that whatever it is he'd share it with me.

He works very hard and brings home less than £30 a week. It must bother him that there isn't much money, especially as he works so hard. When I've paid the rent and bought a little food, there's nothing left. I don't burden him with this; I just get on and manage. He doesn't know that I don't eat. He doesn't know that the vegetable stews I make are from someone's compost heap. It wouldn't serve any purpose to tell him. This quarter's bills are due in and I don't have any money for them. Looks like we'll be up to our necks in debts and red letters. At least I'll have something to light a fire with. I don't give a toss any more. They can cut everything off or blow up the house.

I've explained to Steve that I wouldn't mind having these responsibilities if I had a little gratitude sometimes. A compliment at meal times (that's unfair, my meals are atrocious), a cuddle when I feel sad. Steve says, 'If you want compensations, piss off down the social.' All I'm asking is a little comfort. He won't admit that he needs comfort, love, help, conversation even, from me. As soon as I think I'm getting to know him a bit, he puts up a barrier and it won't budge. How the hell can I like — let alone love — Steve when I don't know him?

Steve, please let me into your heart. I know that you're entitled to secrets, but I only want to be a part of you — for us to be a part of each other. I can't go on pleading and degrading myself to have you as my husband. I've got to get out of this place or I'll go mad. It might take years for Steve to include me in his life. I can't wait years. I do love Steve, but I can't go on much longer being excluded from his life. I told him all about me. I didn't keep anything secret. Don't brush me away. Don't leave me alone and unloved.

Christ, I feel so inadequate. I must mean something to Steve, even if I'm just the old bag that irons his shirts, washes his clothes and makes his bed. I've always been warm and responsive to Steve, but still he doesn't care for me. I'm just an ongoing nutcase.

I need some excitement in my life. I've wasted too much time already. In the local paper today I saw that a film I'd been waiting for was on, so I asked Linda if she'd babysit. Steve and I went out, regardless of money. Why should we work all week and only have money to give to other people? If we don't get out and have a bit of fun we will end up divorced. I'm not a placid housewife who gets thrills from nappies, dishes, hoovering and cleaning.

Steve needs a new pair of shoes. He's only had the others three months and they're useless. The soles go flip, flap. He's walking as though he's got flippers on. I don't care — perhaps if he wears them long enough his mates at work will organize a whip-round. If I could get a full-time job where I could take Sheryl with me, I'd contribute to the household. No doubt I'm a rotten cow, going to the pictures and not buying Steve a pair of shoes. The reason is simple. He goes out to the disco and plays darts every Friday night while I stop home. I don't mind; as I've said before, I trust him implicitly. I could go out, I suppose, but I have nowhere to go and no one to go with. I don't go to pubs because I don't drink.

It's midnight and I'm sitting down for the first time today. Steve's friend Terry called round for the turntable to take to the disco. Steve had the garage key, so as the sun was shining I put Sheryl in her buggy and walked over to Steve's work to get the key. Bruce came too. He's a powerful dog. It takes a lot of energy going walkies. We couldn't part with him, he's so gentle. When it's cold I dress him up in Steve's old shirts; he looks so funny I laugh till I ache. I got back about 4 p.m. I was ravenous, and after I'd fed Sheryl I had bread, cheese and eggs. It made a change from tea and sugar. Steve came home for his stew. After I'd changed Sheryl, bathed her, put her to bed and then washed the dishes, I thought I'd sit down — and then remembered a ton of ironing I had to do.

I've cut down my smoking from 60 a day to 30. That deserves a pat on the back. Pat, pat.

I feel melancholy tonight. I'm not sure why. Why do people say it does you good to cry and gets it off your chest? The only time I get anything off my chest is when I have a good cough.

Today I feel hurt. It's my own fault, but none the less I deserved a smile for what I did. While we were out shopping we went into the shop where Steve bought his shoes. I couldn't bear the flip, flap, flip, flap any longer. In a rather loud voice I said to the manager, 'After six weeks these shoes are a disgrace.' He apologized and refunded the money. We went to another shop further up the precinct and bought another pair the same.

In the second shop we met someone Steve knew and I told him what I'd done. Steve was furious and sulked, calling me 'an old bag'. Next time his shoes wear out he can get himself a refund.

Steve told me last night that however hard he tries he can't do anything. He said he wanted to do things at school but never did because he couldn't.

I asked him, 'What do you want to do?'

'Dunno.' He shrugged his shoulders.

Steve told me he knows he's a nothing and can't be bothered to be a something, because there did not and still does not appear to be any point; so he will just plod on.

'Steve, my love, you must feel so utterly defeated.' Christ, I wish life was just a little easier.

I've been thinking of ways to help Steve. He needs some self-esteem. I've suggested night school to learn a trade. I can't think of anything else. He sits and stares the whole time. I'm talking to myself. I'm seriously thinking of leaving him, but where would I go? St Bernard's is the only place I could go and feel I belong, but they wouldn't let me keep Sheryl. I've got to get out of this mess. I have no right to deprive Sheryl of her daddy, but then why should I stay and make us all even unhappier? In the long run it will be less painful to part from Steve and make a life with Sheryl. Maybe I should leave Sheryl behind. NO — I couldn't desert my baby. I might not be a good wife. But don't ever say I'm a bad mother. I will not leave Sheryl whatever happens.

We've been married two years today and it's snowing like it did on our wedding day. I don't think I'll run away after all. Ann up the road is starting work full-time on Monday. She has asked me if I'll mind her two children, Lisa and Ian. Ian's a little devil, but I can handle him. I've also heard that I can go back to work at the hospital. I'll see how things go looking after the kids, and then consider it.

I'm going to be busy, aren't I?

I'm cracking up. I'm too young to know what to do about all this. I spent years trying to be free, and now I'm free I don't know how to cope. I learnt to accept I was mental. I still wanted to be free. I felt I could get by in the outside world if the doors would open and set me free. When I got out I met Steve and fell in love. We married after four years. I loved him so much that I shared everything with him. He knows all my secrets and soft spots. Now I have nothing to fall back on. I don't even have my pride. I mustn't cry. Crying is a weakness and I'm an adult now. Steve doesn't want me any more. I've tried everything I know to try to save our marriage.

Now I'm back to square one. I'm not a girl any more. I'm a young woman with a baby to look after. I'm not in a mental home with lots of people around. Instead I'm on my own, with no one's arms to comfort me, no one's ears to listen to my sadness. I'm locked up in solitary confinement in my own private mental home.

I'm having a mental breakdown — can you hear me? Yoooo, hoooo.

11

WHO WAS I

When I went into St Bernard's I think I had all my faculties. Mother says she knew everything that went on — but she didn't know what happened when she wasn't there. She got reports from the ward Sisters, but they only worked there, they didn't live there with the dread and anguish. Lots of incidents they closed their eyes to.

The first lesbian attack I suffered made me so disgusted and ashamed I didn't tell my mother. Even when I tried to shock her I never spoke of sex between women. I don't even think to this day I have told my mum what happened; I would be much too ashamed.

After I'd left St Bernard's, sometimes when I saw a woman in the street I'd get a funny feeling in my tummy. I wasn't unduly worried, but I did wonder why a woman would make me feel like that, especially when I didn't know her.

I never spoke to anyone about this. At that time I hadn't had any heterosexual relationships, and the relationship I had had with Linda in 19s didn't appear to be the same thing I experienced with these women at a distance. I didn't consider it sexual, because my experiences of lesbian sex were of viciousness and brute force. Nor did I see that what I did with Linda was sex. It was sex, there's no denying it, but I went to Linda because I loved her and she made me feel loved and protected. Our relationship developed into something good during the time we knew each other. I knew she didn't need me like I needed her, even though she would have killed anyone who hurt me. She was extremely jealous and yet she wasn't a lesbian.

Gladys was Nellie's crony. She was short and fat, with an

oval face, snow-white hair and the cockneyest of accents. Her nose was badly stained with snuff. Gladys always wore the same clothes, except for her pinafore which she changed every day.

'Gladys, what's that? Let us have some.'

'Piss off, kid,' she hissed. When she spoke she pushed her neck out so far she looked like a tortoise.

I shuffled off, mumbling, 'Silly old tortoise-neck.'

Nellie called after me, 'I've got some, kid.'

I was delighted.

'Put your head back and sniff hard, like this,' and Nellie demonstrated. She held the back of my neck and kept her finger and thumb up my nose until I screamed. I sneezed and sneezed. It felt like it was at the back of my throat and in my mouth.

'No more, Nellie. Get off, I don't want any more.'

She pushed me away roughly. It was awful stuff. I wished I hadn't asked for any, but I got so bored caged up in 19s all day. Besides, anyone who was anyone snuffed snuff, so why shouldn't I?

Some weeks Miss Bates, the occupational therapist, would come. I knitted my brother Fred a jumper with a cable pattern. I also made him a Snoopy dog and a kangaroo with a baby in its pouch. The baby kangaroo was about an inch and a half long, and I kept it when I gave the mother kangaroo to Fred.

One night, after lights out, I was lying in bed feeling mischievous, playing with the baby kangaroo. I was telling it I was pissed off and in a squeaky voice it talked to me. I could hear Doris snoring loudly and thought I'd have some fun. Doris was another inmate who was built like the side of a house. She had short brown hair, deep-set eyes with fat folds and her teeth were decayed. She was short, with round shoulders, and her body leant heavily to the right.

She was lying on her back, mouth wide open, snoring and grunting. I crept over to her bed and turned back the covers. I lifted her nightie and her 46-inch bosom and put the baby kangaroo under her bosom. The smell from under her bosom was diabolical and I dropped it. I went back to my own bed,

71

thinking I would retrieve the kangaroo in the morning before Doris woke up.

In the morning when I looked under Doris's tit the kangaroo was gone. I know Doris didn't know he was there; she'd been fast asleep. I could only surmise that someone had watched me go through that daft procedure, then waited until I'd gone to sleep and nicked baby kangaroo for herself. I never saw him again; also I never messed around with other people's tits after that.

Poor old Doris was an incurable what? I don't think even the doctors knew. She shuffled around at an incredibly slow pace, saying over and over, 'I'm all confused in my head. I'm all mixed up in the brainpits. I'm all tied up in Dr Lindsay's trousers.' This incessant rambling was a constant source of fun for me. I would tease Doris wickedly until she shrieked her ramblings louder. To this day if I can't remember something I mimic Doris shuffling along saying, 'I'm all mixed up in the brainpits.'

Her husband never came to see her. She had twins, a boy and a girl, who were at university. If ever they heard me mimicking their mother they would get furious and tell me off. I thought they were as potty as their mother. At a distance I teased them too.

When the weather was fine, all the patients would be herded together and under guard trooped down the back stairs for 'some fresh air'. When you've been in a place like this and are given pills three times a day, and have no stimulation except for violent sexual assaults, you become slow and dummified. Even the nurses found it an effort to cajole us into doing anything. It appeared to me that it made life easier for them to let us sit and vegetate.

Down the back stairs in single file. Heads counted as you went. Nearly all the inmates had been there so long that it was like their home, so escape wasn't even considered by them. I was always made to stay close to a nurse, because I would bugger off if the opportunity arose.

Being in the courtyard was the same as being in the ward. Nothing to do. Lots of old women sitting happily with their hands in their laps, fixed grins on their faces and saliva encrusted at the edges of their mouths. Christ, I couldn't see the point. It was all such a waste of time.

One day my mother came down to the courtyard with us. When we were all being rounded up to go back to the ward, Mum said, 'Right, Shue, I'll see you in a couple of weeks, now be a good girl and I might write out a pass for the weekend.' She gave me a kiss and walked off.

A nurse ran after her and grabbed her by the arm. 'Where do you think you're going?'

'I'm going home, dear.'

'Oh no you're not. Not while I'm in charge.'

'But my lift, dear. I'll miss my lift,' said Mum, getting agitated.

The nurse escorted Mum back to the ward with a firm grip on her arm.

'Hey, Mum, she thinks you're one of us,' I teased.

When we got back to the ward, the nurse said to Dickinson, 'This one thought she was going home. I soon sorted her out.'

Sister laughed and apologized to my mother.

I remember thinking if the nurses couldn't tell the difference between us, then there couldn't be a noticeable difference. If they emptied the mental homes on to the streets for a few hours, I bet they'd find it hard to round us up without making a few mistakes.

I wanted my ears pierced. I found a rusty old brooch that was Doris's, and stood in front of a mirror. I stuck the dirty brooch-pin through my ear lobes. I got a darning needle from Sister and threaded a piece of cotton through the holes. I walked around pulling on the cotton to keep the holes open until Nurse Bates brought me in a pair of sleepers.

A number of the women decided they wanted their ears pierced too. So for two cigarettes I pierced their ears. I had done about 10 pairs of ear lobes before anyone noticed. Sister Hutchins went berserk and called Matron James. Matron was really pretty but a right old nag-bag.

'Read, what do you think you're doing?'

'Making holes in their ears. Look, like this,' and I showed her mine.

'I can see that. What if someone got an infection, what would you do then?'

'Wait till they got better and do it again.'

She thrust herself forward, growling, and clipped my ear. 'Get out, and no more ear-piercing.'

Everyone who'd had it done was pleased. I hadn't managed to fit Sarah in before I was caught. I told her that when the heat had died down I would do hers, but she wanted them done then and I refused. She kept on and on about it for a couple of days; then she tripped me up as I walked past and kicked me in the stomach. It was so unexpected that I was winded and couldn't retaliate.

Matron James was standing by, gloating. 'Look where you're walking, Read.'

'Mad bitch,' I shouted at her.

She didn't pay any heed, but once I was on my feet she hit me across the back of my head and knocked me clean off balance again. 'That might teach you not to call people names.'

I gave up ear-piercing after that.

When Mum came to visit, she didn't like taking me out in the grounds because I did naughty things.

There was an old man in ragged clothes who roamed the grounds looking for dog-ends. He shuffled along with his head bowed like everyone else did. The first time, I had already passed him when I stopped, eyes wide open. I turned and ran back in front of him to see if what I had seen was right. My mother told me years later that she had seen it long before we even reached him and prayed silently that I wouldn't notice.

Sure enough, there hanging out of his trousers was his penis. I might have been young but I knew it was one hell of a winkle. It was the first one I had ever seen. I just stood mesmerized.

He shuffled along with two fingers pressed up to his lips as if smoking a cigarette. He gathered up all the dog-ends. When he had a sizeable hoard he split them up and made a fag. Most of the inmates did this. Some didn't bother to take the tobacco out; they'd put the filthy dog-end in their mouths and go begging for a light. The first time I saw this done it annoyed me; it looked so pointless — there was only the cork tip left — but it wasn't long before I was doing the same thing.

I pushed my mother towards the old man, saying, 'Go on Mum, now's your chance, fancy some of that?'

My mother was terrified. She tried to get away, but I was too strong and maintained a firm grip on her arm. The old man was only interested in a dog-end. 'Gissa fag, lady,' or if he had a dog-end in his mouth he'd say, 'Gissa light, lady.'

My mum was so frightened and repulsed she'd give him the whole packet just to make him go away. After this he got clever, and each time he saw my mum he'd wander over saying, 'Fags, lady. Gissa fag.' When Mother pretended not to hear he'd sidle up to her, rubbing his limp penis. Needless to say he got the whole packet again.

He didn't fancy my mum; he only wanted a cigarette, but I didn't tell her that. He certainly had a whopper.

Sylvia had only been out of the pads for two days when she decided against all the rules that she was going to have a cigarette before breakfast. Sylvia did things in such a way that it was impossible not to see what she was doing. She had a fast, determined way of moving that drew your eyes towards her. Even though I loved Sylvia, I can't say I condone what she did to Gran Hutchins, but by the same token I feel the staff could have handled it differently.

No one had matches, for obvious reasons. The only place to obtain a light was from the pilot-light on the water-heater in the kitchen. I saw Sylvia flounce across the length of the ward making her intentions obvious. Gran Hutchins, Staff Appleby and another nurse followed her. Sylvia had already got a light, and as they approached her she upturned the two-tier trolley full of the breakfast crockery. As they'd cornered her, she used the chair beside her as a shield and hurled anything that came to hand to ward them off. Edging her way out of the kitchen, she went back to the dormitory, sat on her bed and finished the cigarette.

The alarm had been raised and help arrived. Six nurses crashed into the dormitory, dragged Sylvia from her bed and made their way towards the pads. There was a nurse on each arm — Staff Appleby behind and Gran Hutchins in front. The other two nurses went ahead to open the pads. They managed all right until they got to the glass partition which separated the dormitory from the living area.

The nurse on the right-hand side had to let go of Sylvia's arm to get through. Then Sylvia smashed her right arm through the glass while the nurse, Staff Appleby and Gran were still pulling her along. I saw Sylvia kick out at Gran and she caught her in the side with her toe. I suspect the pain from her arm made her do this. Gran was hurt and dropped to the floor. The staff let go of Sylvia and helped Gran. Blood was gushing out of Sylvia's arm. She sat down cross-legged and watched the blood pump out of her arm. I put my arms around her and sobbed. She thought I was hurt and stroked my hair.

Sylvia and Gran were both taken to Middlesex General Hospital. Sylvia came back to 18s the following day. Her arm was in an awful state; it hung down like a cripple's and was totally useless. She couldn't even move her fingers. Gran wasn't so lucky. She died about 10 days later. She had been in intensive care; Sylvia had damaged her kidneys when she'd kicked her. Not long after, Sylvia was moved to another mental hospital.

I missed Gran and her ability to control the ward. But I missed Sylvia more. I loved her even though she spent most of her time hurting herself and others. She never physically hurt me, but I spent lots of hours hurting when she had done something so dreadful to herself that once again she was in the pads. I never saw Sylvia again. When I tried to talk about her, I was met with a wall of silence.

There was the one doctor called Dr Lovett who came every week. He was about five feet 10 inches tall, and bald except for a thin line of hair round the back of his head. His lips were thin, his nose was long and his eyes were expressionless. He was in every aspect an idiot. I thought that the years of working there had taken their toll. When he came on the ward and tried to relock the main door, a crowd of at least 20 women flocked towards him. He would leap towards the office, hopping on alternate legs, his shoulders hunched, with his head lolling on to his shoulder in an imbecile fashion.

Dr Lovett annoyed and infuriated me. Anyone could manipulate him to write out a pass to a drug conference or to give them a signed document of sanity. I only remember three interviews with him — that made less than one a year — while I was on 19s. I invariably lost my temper with him and ended by calling him some degenerate name, and I got a smack round the ear from Sister when I left the office.

With his mouth gaping open for at least two minutes he would ask me, 'And have we had a nice day today?' His mouth would close and he'd lean forward, hands in his lap and a ridiculous grin on his face. It makes me cross even now to think of him. I don't know if he retired or whether he was admitted to the male equivalent of 19s, but suddenly he didn't come anymore. Thank God. But . . . I didn't bargain for who took his place.

Her name was Dr Walker and she had short, bob-style hair. She was tall and slim, with the hardest, cruellest face I had ever seen. I despised her. Her nature was harder than her features. She only saw the patients she wanted to see — which consisted every day of Pauline the rapist.

Sister Dickinson announced not long after Gran died that she was retiring. At this stage my life in St Bernard's was totally out of control. With Gran dying, Sister retiring, Dr Walker moving in, Sylvia gone, I couldn't see any point. All my security was suddenly gone. I got violent. If someone bumped into me I beat them. When I wasn't fighting I was sitting in a corner. I hated my mother for putting me there. I hated my father for dying. And I hated me.

The week before Sister left I started 'smashing' (knocking out windows). The sound of breaking glass really relieves the tension. Smashing became like a drug once I'd started. I didn't want to hurt myself, I just wanted relief. The sound felt so good after the deadly silence I thought existed in my head. I wasn't very well.

After I'd been smashing at every opportunity I got, Sister took me into her office and talked to me. She was so kind I nearly cried. She told me she liked me and had great faith that one day I would be outside, leading a normal life. I told her how unhappy and confused I was and how sad I felt that she was retiring.

I talked and she listened. I had always thought how hard and cruel she was, but that day I realized that she couldn't be soft-hearted and maintain control on the ward. I told her I wanted to sleep and forget; not to hear all the rantings and sexual goings-on all night. I wanted to unwind. Sister gave me an injection of paraldehyde which knocked me out for 24 hours. It hurt like hell, but I didn't care; I just wanted to sleep. When I woke up, nothing had changed — in fact it was even worse. Sister Daley took Sister's place.

I begged my mum to take me home. I wanted out. I couldn't keep any food down. When I smelt food I was physically sick. It was a wonder I didn't have any hypos. I was living solely on my nerves. Whereas before all the changes I had just been a young girl, now I was a nervous wreck. I was losing weight. This went on for two months, and then my mum took me home 'on trial' to see how I fitted in with the family.

I withdrew from people. I wouldn't talk, because my head was thinking so fast I thought my words would trip over themselves. I lost more weight. I was only allowed home because my mother signed me out and took full responsibility for me. She never let me out of her sight for a minute. I wanted to die, but the pills and anything else that I could have committed suicide with mysteriously disappeared. I didn't have the energy to search for anything, so I settled for sleep. I couldn't keep track of time. I don't even recall how long I was at home. I do remember feeling that home was even worse than St Bernard's.

I wondered and fretted how I would ever be able to live and

cope in the outside world. My mind raced through questions and whys and wherefores, but I didn't have any answers. If only it would all go away. How could I confide in anyone when I didn't even know what I was thinking? It didn't make any sense.

While I was asleep my mum had popped out for 'one of my minutes.' I woke up and made myself a cup of coffee. One minute I was sitting at the kitchen table, drinking my coffee, and the next I was kneeling on the kitchen floor with my hands together, praying to God to help me, to take away my life and give me peace of mind. I had gone over the top. God seemed the only one to turn to, even though I didn't believe in God.

On hearing the noise, my sister Pauline came into the kitchen, and seeing me in that strange position she screamed at me, 'You're mad. You're fucking mad.'

Confirmation was all I needed. I ran out of the house and down the street. I didn't know and I didn't care where I was going. I just ran. I couldn't hear my mum calling me or see anything in front of me. Each time I ran across the road I nearly got run over. I was determined to get away from everything — my life, St Bernard's, my mum — and most of all I was in a blind panic running away from me.

It was pouring with rain, and I was saturated to the skin by the time Mum and Mr Chilton caught up with me. I had a bath and a cup of tea and went to bed. When my mum came up at about 11 p.m., I awoke and told her I wanted to go back to St Bernard's the next day as I couldn't cope with being out. I said I should be where I belonged. St Bernard's was my home and I wanted to go back.

I was shocked when Mum said she knew how I felt and didn't want me to go back. She said I could stay and she would look after me until I was better. I looked at my mum's face and saw how strained she looked. I didn't want to hurt her any more; she had enough worry with the rest of the family, so I would go back.

Next morning I got up and prepared myself to return to St Bernard's. Mum went to see the health visitor who would take us in her car. When I'd packed all my things, Mum said I could sleep in her bed until Miss Carter came. Mum made my favourite lunch — fried cod in batter with chips and peas. As soon as I sat at the table I was retching. Mum was really worried about my not being able to eat.

Miss Carter arrived and I went back to St Bernard's for another two years.

12

AN OPEN WARD

Owing to my lack of secondary education, I was worried about how I would ever get a job. Even though I was ill, I knew that my only chance of freedom was being able to get a job and support myself.

When I had gone home with Mum 'on trial', 18s had been bedlam. When I returned it was a hell-hole. As my mum was leaving, she said, 'Shue, if you want to come home with me, just say so. I'll take you home.'

I knew I had to stay. This was where I belonged. I'd become mentally ill, and the right place to be was a mental hospital. When the doors had slammed shut I unpacked my belongings. I shuffled around, resigned to the fact that this was my home now, and strangely I felt an odd kind of security.

My hair began to fall out. I was becoming so thin I was almost unrecognizable. To this day my hair still hasn't grown properly. After what seemed an eternity I managed to eat a little and I even smiled sometimes at the pathetic goings-on. I gradually became less aggressive. I felt more able to cope with being locked away. To me at that time the prospect of ever being anywhere other than 18s appeared very grim. The thought of living in the outside world panicked me so much that I would fall into an old red chair and shake until I nearly blacked out.

The picture of me in my mind's eye is horrifying to me now. I was tall and thin. I shuffled along without lifting my head, my shoulders bent over, my head bowed and my arms hanging down by my sides. My head was covered with bald patches, and the hair I had was thin and wispy. My face was gaunt and my eyes were staring and set far back in my head. I looked awful. I was told I looked more like 30 than 14.

I still went to Linda's bed. I thought at first she would reject me as I was so ugly inside and outside. I couldn't see any harm in our love for each other — and still can't. I still hated everyone, and if anyone talked to me or tried to be kind I was deeply suspicious. Apart from Linda I only talked to Cynthia. It had not been long since Sylvia had gone, but I couldn't recall what she looked like or how her voice sounded.

One day I wrote a letter to Dr Baruch, the senior consultant. I told him what had been happening to me and how I felt about being on 18s. I asked one of the nurses to post the letter for me. I didn't think she would, but she obviously did. I cornered her one day and called her filthy names. I didn't tell her why. I harboured lots of nasty things in my mind that didn't exist.

Nearly a month later I was approached by two nurses and told, 'Come on, Read, we're going for a walk.'

I sat in my old red chair ignoring them. They stood on either side of me and wrenched me out of the chair by my upper arms. 'Fuck your mother,' I screamed at them.

Under firm escort I was taken to Ellis Ward. I was ushered into Sister's office, and sitting behind the desk was Dr Baruch. He told the nurses he would be quite a while. They could return to their ward and when he had finished he would ring them to come and fetch me. 'Sit down, Miss Read.'

I sat down.

He produced my letter and said, 'When I read this I judged you wanted to see me.'

My mind was panicking. Why was he being so nice? I was suspicious. I found people easier to cope with when they were nasty and unkind to me. 'I only wanted to tell someone how I felt,' I said, my eyes down.

'Well, come on. I'm listening.' He smiled at me.

I told him everything. I swore as part of my defence. He didn't mention my use of swear words. He sat listening and did some writing.

When I'd finished he continued to write and I got shaky. I started to regret writing him the letter. He stopped writing,

looked at me and frowned. 'Miss Read, why are you so thin?'
He said he would see what he could do to alleviate my
situation. He told me I could go.

'Will you ring for the nurses?'

'You know the way. Go on, off you go.'

I ran all the way back to 18s on my own. I was afraid of
getting caught out on my own. When I reached the main door
I felt desperate. It was the first time I had been out of 18s in
three months. It didn't occur to me to run away. I fell back
into the same old routine on 18s.

A fortnight later I was ordered to have my belongings ready
after lunch as I was moving.

'Where?'

'None of yours, Read.'

I plagued one of the nurses and finally she told me it was
Ward 17. Ward 17 had become an open ward only recently. I
panicked again. How would I cope? I'd been locked up for too
long. I wouldn't be able to resist the temptation to run if
something upset me. To this day I'm impulsive. If I feel trapped
I find it awfully difficult not to run away.

That morning Sister Daley prodded me, saying, 'What
makes you think you're so different, Read? You're the same as
all the others, mad as a hatter.' She didn't leave me alone for a
minute. How I didn't hit her or give her a filthy mouthful I'll
never know. Now I know that she made me more determined
to show the likes of her just how far I could get once I was out
of 18s. Sister Daley and her staff were poor substitutes for
Sister Dickinson and dear old Gran.

I made lots of mistakes once I was moved. But I never did go
back into 18s as a patient. Though Ward 17 was an open
ward, the irony was it was only one step away from 18s. I was
acutely aware that if I put a foot wrong I would simply be
thrown back into 18s. I reckoned they must have trusted me
more than I did myself. However hard I tried I couldn't see
this move ending in anything but failure for me.

By 2 p.m. I was a patient on Ward 17. I had my own room,
which I greatly appreciated. There were a few patients I'd
known on Ellis Ward. It was funny, because there was me

moving away from 18s and them moving towards it.

Sister Cahn was in charge on 17s and she was gorgeous — so kind and thoughtful, unlike Sister Daley. Sister Cahn always made time for me. Best of all, she treated me like a human being with feelings. 'Come and be making me laugh, Sue,' she would say. Whenever she had tea she ordered a tray for two. I told her what happened on 19s and 18s. But I made light of it so's it sounded funny. It took a lot to make light of those years that had been so painful.

My mum came to visit, expecting to find me still on 18s. The last time I'd seen her I'd still been very ill. She was really happy and gave me a little lecture. 'Now Shue, it's all up to you, you can stay out of there if you behave. And I know you can be good if you try.' The more people lectured me, the more determined I became to get out of St Bernard's and never look back.

Mum took me shopping to Southall High Street. We did some window shopping. My hair was still quite sparse, and keeping control of my temper when the patients mocked me was hard. So we went into a hairdresser's salon and leafed through a book of modern styles. The majority were all beehive fashions, except the close-cropped Judy Driscoll style.

My hair looked so much better. I was really grateful to Mum. When we got back, Sister hugged me and said, 'Sue, you're looking like convict 99, sure you are. But you're really beautiful.' We all laughed. When I ran my hands over my head, my hair moved straight back into place. The bald patches couldn't be seen as my hair was only a quarter of an inch long all over my head.

I still smelt like a skunk. Sister would gently coax me to bath. '99, you're not smelling as pretty as you're looking.'

'Leave me alone,' I'd mumble. After all, I couldn't smell anything.

There were about 32 patients on 17s, so if anyone wanted a bath they could have one without supervision. I liked the freedom to come and go more or less as I pleased. I asked Sister for the bath keys one day and went for a bath — my first bath for almost three years. I lounged in the lovely hot water for ages — my own water, nice and fresh, and when it got a bit cold I just filled it up with more hot water. There were no one's eyes prying on me. Since the breakdown in 18s had left me so skinny, I was totally flat-chested. It was terrific to have privacy. I didn't like having my hair or body mocked.

Every day I went to art therapy. The building was made of light-green planks of wood. It was in the grounds, set a little away from the wards. The woman in charge was Mrs Manuilow; she was Polish. She was an artist and sculptress. She was highly strung and flappy. She waved her arms frantically when she spoke; if she was in a hurry her arms became just a blur.

The man who helped her was Mr Smith. He was ginger-haired with a ginger moustache and beard. He had a large paunch that hung over his trousers. He was a clever man, but more peculiar. I would make suggestive advances to him. He was daftly coy and blushed deeply. I'd creep up behind him and pinch his bum, or put the palm of my hand between his legs — like goosing, but much more forward. 'Gissa kiss,' I'd say, puckering my lips. I was cruel and made him look even dafter than he was.

Art therapy was there to express your feelings. Instead of smashing, I would go and throw paint all over the board. I wasn't in the least artistic, but I really enjoyed myself. I liked making all that mess and not being punished.

My mother came with me sometimes when she visited on Tuesdays. She would get cross and embarrassed at the things I did and said to Mr Smith. After a while he began retaliating. He'd touch my bum and I'd say loudly, 'Would you mind leaving my arse alone, you dirty old sod.' He'd stand there with his arms by his sides, looking flushed. When we were on our way back to 17s, Mum would say, 'One day, Shue, one day.'

'What you on about?' I'd nudge her. She really annoyed me when she used that 'I know what I'm talking about' tone to me.

Brenda was the only patient who had a nurse with her when

85

she went to art therapy. She was in Ward 9, the ward below 18s. She had been in St Bernard's for years and was about 39 years old. She was violent and would lash out for no apparent reason. She screamed continuously about fucks and cunts. She'd throw back her head and scream out the most perverted sexual things. One day, while her nurse was in the loo, she went up behind Mr Smith and tried to strangle him with her used sanitary towel. She made me nervous. Just before I left St Bernard's for the last time, Brenda died of a brain haemorrhage.

Mr Lucas also went to art therapy. He never painted or did anything there except make the tea. He smoked this stinking old pipe. He was about 55 years old and had also been there for years. Across the front of his head he had a long scar. Mr Smith said he'd had a lobotomy. According to Mr Smith there was a 50-50 chance of success with this operation. It didn't seem to have made Mr Lucas anything. He was reasonably placid. Occasionally he'd stand up and shout about something that no one could understand, but I never knew him to be violent. Sometimes he would sit and masturbate. This really fascinated me. As he was in a glazed state while he did this, I would sit next to him and watch at close quarters. When he'd ejaculated he'd wipe the sperm on his upper trouser-legs. His trousers were white and crusty. He always wore the same suit. He walked by lifting his left shoulder and left leg together and dragging the right leg along, like a child negotiates stairs. His eyes were close together, with bushy eyebrows; his nose was long, with flaring nostrils. His top lip was thin, the lower lip large, protruding and badly cracked. His voice was loud and crackly like a poorly tuned radio.

Rex was an old hippie of about 40. His hair was long at the back and sparse on top. He was unkempt and smelt nasty. His only conversation was about sex. His persistent pawing me drove me mad. On one occasion I kneed him in the balls when he'd cornered me behind an easel at art therapy. This course of action did not deter him; if anything he became even more suggestive.

There was also a collection of old ladies who could have been sisters from a large family. They weren't. But their facial expressions and physical mannerisms were so alike they looked as though they'd been cloned. They weren't old, but they looked old. Their clothes were long to their ankles. The dresses were of loud garish prints, and they wore stockings that only came to the knee and were held there by elastic bands. The shoes were men's lace-up brogues. They all wore a pink or green headscarf, summer and winter.

Lena was Italian — short and fat, with a round face, large eyes and thick lashes, a long nose and full lips. She had an enormous backside, and whenever she saw a man she would wiggle it provocatively. She would say, 'Mens like-a the big bum.'

I began going to the social on Ellis Ward every Thursday night. I loved it. It was great to get back to dancing and have a little night-life. When it was time for refreshments, if I went to take a biscuit, Lena would shriek in her hysterical fashion, arms waving, 'Suzie, you not eatta the biscuit, you diabeteech.' She was so loud. I couldn't get away with eating anything while she was around.

I can't recall how long I was on Ward 17 but it seemed a long time. My time there was untroubled and happy. Sister Cahn was kindness itself, and I started trusting people again. One day Sister called me into her office. '99, me old darling, you're moving in the morning.'

'I'm not. I'm staying here with you.'

She put her arm on my shoulder and when I looked up at her I saw her eyes were misty. I remember thinking, she likes me.

'I'm not going nowhere, I'm stopping with you.' I flung my arms round her waist and nestled my head, fighting to hold back my tears.

'Dr Morrish wants you to move over to Connolly.'

'Dr Morrish?' I went weak. I hadn't seen him for years. 'Where's Connolly?'

'Well away from the main building, 99.'

'I will come and see you.'

'You'll be getting ready, 99, off you go.'

I left her office. I couldn't believe it, I'd be seeing Dr Morrish again. Everything was moving too fast. Connolly was a lot more than one step away from 18s. Could I cope?

13

STARTING WORK

My stomach was full of butterflies as we approached Connolly Ward. I'd said goodbye to Sister Cahn and promised to visit her often. I wondered if Dr Morrish would remember me. I bet he wouldn't. I was nervous and hoped this move was the right thing for me.

We went straight into Sister's office. Sister Innes was on duty. She was short and fat. Her hair was whitey-grey, short and curly. I could tell that she had false teeth and only wore them if she had to, because her mouth was shrivelled and when she spoke there was a dry clicking noise. The nurse introduced me to Sister Innes.

'I'll have no trouble from you in my ward, Susan. Is that understood?'

'Yes, Sister.' She hates me. It's not going to work here, I thought.

A nurse showed me to my bed. I put my things in the bedside locker and went to look around. As you came in through the main door there was a long corridor with doors on either side. The first door on the left was a bathroom and toilet. Sister's office was next. Then came Dr Morrish's office, and next door was a waiting-room with armchairs. On the right the first door was the kitchen. Then there was the linen room, and next door a consulting-room with a bed and portable screen.

At the end of the corridor was a TV room with armchairs. To the right of the corridor was the dining area, and on from there was a small dormitory with eight beds with lockers beside them. My bed was on the left-hand side, third bed along. At the bottom end of the dormitory were two large

double doors. Behind these were a bathroom, toilet and two
sinks. To the left of the corridor was a carpeted sitting area
with pot-plants and a record-player. Further on were a
dormitory and bathing area identical to the ones on the other
side.

After looking around and finding where things were, I went
to the main door and opened it. I looked behind me and saw
Sister Innes watching me. I closed the door and went back
down the corridor. I made sure Sister's office was closed and
she wasn't around before I opened the door again. I pulled
down the handle and looked around; seeing no one I stepped
outside. It was a strange feeling opening a main door. It took a
few days to get used to how things were done away from the
main building.

When I saw Dr Morrish my head wouldn't think straight.

'Hello Sue, how are you?'

'Er um, fine.'

'Good. Have you made yourself at home?'

'Yes. She hates me.'

'Who hates you?'

'Sister, old Innesy.'

'Sue, I think your reputation got here before you. Sister is
really very nice. I'm sure you'll get on well together.'

'How long am I here for?'

'That's up to you, Sue. The next move should be home.'

'I can't go home. I don't fit in.'

'We'll see, Sue.'

My first night was good. I walked round the grounds before
I went to bed. Next morning I put on my dressing-gown and
went into the living area. Josie and Janet were talking. I
interrupted them. Josie said, 'Clear off, kid. I'm in here to get
some peace from kids.'

'Bollocks.' I went and got washed and dressed. I asked
Doreen in the bed next to me for a cigarette. I went in the
toilets. Old habits die hard. We weren't allowed to smoke
before breakfast in the main building.

After breakfast sister showed me the rota pinned up behind
the kitchen door. There were certain duties that were mine for

that week. She explained that the duties varied from week to week.

Sister Williams was the other duty Sister. She was Welsh, as her name suggests. She was short and fat with a soft, pretty face, even though she must have been 50. My mother and Willie got on well together. She liked me and showed it.

Even though I was in Connolly, I still found myself tripping up the stairs to Ward 17. Sister Cahn was always pleased to see me and welcomed me with a cup of tea. 'I'll be thinking you'll be glad to see the back of us, 99.'

'No, Innesy hates me and I miss you.'

One day Sister Cahn said it was best if I didn't visit her too often as it didn't look good.

'Whatcha mean, good?'

'You don't belong here now, 99.'

'I don't belong anywhere. They hate me there and now you hate me too.'

'99, I'll never hate you, me old darling.' She put her arms round me and held me close. She told me that since I was out of the main building I should look to the future and maybe get myself a job, earn some money and move towards living outside. I promised I wouldn't come to see her any more. I kissed her goodbye.

'Dr Morrish, I want to get a job.' I was expecting him to say 'No' and was prepared to shout and holler if necessary.

'What were you thinking of doing, Sue?'

'Dunno. Will you give me a reference?'

He reached for pen and paper. He wrote me a reference on St Bernard's notepaper, starting with 'To whom it may concern'. He handed me the reference and I read it. He had said such nice things about me. Before I went to sleep that night I thought, I won't let him down. He's got more faith in me than I have. I really love him.

Next morning I got up and had breakfast. Dr Morrish had lent me £1 for the bus fares. I caught the bus opposite the gates into Greenford. The bus dropped me outside Tesco's. I went in and asked to see the manager. Once in his office I produced the reference, which he read, and asked if I could start on Monday. My wages would be £7.10s. a week. I'd have one day off a week, but I must always work Saturdays.

I couldn't believe it. I dashed back to Connolly, bumping into Innesy as I bounced in the door.

'No running on my ward, Susan.'

'I've got a job, I've got a job,' I squealed.

'No screeching on my ward.'

I ran down the corridor, turning left into the living area. 'I've got a job.'

No one wanted to share my joy.

'Where's Dr Morrish?' I asked Innesy.

'He's not here.'

'Very clever. I can see that. Where is he?'

'Out of here, I'm busy.'

'Don't smile, will you? You might crack your ugly mug.'

She pushed the door closed in my face.

Dr Morrish came that evening. I ran up to him. 'I've got a job.'

He hugged me. When I went into his office he lightly scolded me for being rude to Innesy. At least Dr Morrish and Willie were pleased I'd got a job, even if it was only filling shelves at Tesco's.

I waited ages for a bus on Monday morning. I only just made the 8.30 a.m. start. The manager asked a girl called Gloria to show me around and get me an overall. Gloria was of medium height, with a beehive hair-do. She had piercing eyes and a long nose. Her bosom was large as was her bum, and she had thick ankles and legs. When we were in the canteen and I'd taken off my coat to put on the overall, she said in her common voice, 'Gawd, girl, you ain't 'arf skinny.' I hung my head and buttoned up my overall.

Though I'd been taken on as a shelf-filler, I ended up working in the meat department, packing meat and covering it with clingfilm. I was sitting on my own in the small canteen at lunchtime. At the table in front of me were Gloria and her friend June. Gloria said, 'You married, girl?'

'No.'

'How old are you, girl?'

'Guess,' I said, offended.

'Twenty-eight? Thirty?'

I couldn't believe it. Did I really look that old? 'No, I'm 15½.'

'Jesus girl, whatcha done to yourself?' Gloria turned to June and said my being 15 accounted for the fact I had 'no titties'.

'You leave my tits alone.'

'Awright girl, keep ya 'air on.'

They finished their lunch and left the canteen. I moved my seat to behind the door. I was leafing through the newspapers when someone sat down at my table and said, 'Fancy going to the flicks tonight?'

'Er, no thanks.'

'Go on, it's a good film.'

'No thanks.' I could imagine his reaction when after asking to take me home I led him to St Bernard's.

'Suit yourself.' He moved to another table.

About a week later I was late getting to work because the bus was delayed and I could hear jeering and laughing upstairs. I went up the stairs two at a time, hoping no one noticed I was late. In the back of a delivery lorry was Kenny, who was an object of fun to everyone. He had blond hair and a white face, scared eyes and pouty lips. Both the men and the women played nasty tricks on Kenny. This time they'd removed his trousers and underpants and thrown them on top of the lorry. He was inside the empty lorry sitting on his knees, pulling down his shirt to cover his private parts. I felt sorry for him and said angrily, 'Give him back his trousers.'

'If ya want 'im to 'ave 'is trousers, ya'd better get 'em, girl,' smirked Gloria.

So I did. I shinned up the side of the lorry to retrieve his trousers. With my first week's wages I'd bought myself a couple of miniskirts and tops. The men were making a hell of a noise, wolf-whistling and urging me on. I got Kenny's trousers but I couldn't reach his underpants. The manager was cross when I came down and berated me about being there only a couple of weeks and already displaying myself to all and sundry.

It became a regular occurrence for Graham (the boy who'd asked me to the flicks) to sit at my table at tea breaks and lunchtimes. He was nice-looking. He had his hair short on top and long round his shoulders at the back. His eyes were deep-set, his nose long and his mouth full. He was quite tall and lean. He always wore a torn green parka and bovver boots. It was nice to have a boy show interest in me. I began thinking that if I lived at my mum's I'd be able to go to the flicks with Graham.

'Dr Morrish, can I go home?'

'Why?'

'There's a boy who wants to go out with me. I don't want him to know I live here.'

'I've no objections, but you'll have to ask your mum.'

I asked for a pass so I could see my mum after work. I asked her if I could move back home. She didn't like the idea. 'We'll try weekends first, we will, Shue.'

I sighed, but it would have to do. At least I'd be able to go out with Graham at weekends.

'Good film on tonight, Sue.'

'Really?'

'Come with us, Sue. I'll walk you home after.'

'All right.' I rang my mum and told her I wouldn't be home until about 11 p.m.

Graham lived in Northolt. I wouldn't let him take me home; I made him leave me at South Ruislip train station. He didn't kiss me or hold my hand. He asked me out again at lunchtime the next day. He said as it was Saturday we could go to a disco and stay out a bit longer. We had a great evening. He left me at the station at about 11.45 p.m. and I was home by midnight. I didn't see him on the Sunday. Sunday evening I put my toothbrush and other things into a carrier bag and went back to St Bernard's for the week. It had been a good weekend without any trouble.

Graham couldn't understand why I wouldn't go out with him during the week and wouldn't let him walk me home at weekends. After going out with him for four weekends I took him home. We sat in the kitchen while Mum and the family sat in the living-room. He still hadn't kissed me, yet he asked me to sit on his lap. I could feel the pressure of him against my upper leg. He asked if I'd ever been manipulated. I shrugged and said I didn't know what he meant. He explained that manipulation was the female version of masturbation. I said, 'No.'

He was 17 and knew more about some things than I did.

One day he took me to his house. It was a town house with three floors. He warned me before we went in to be very quiet. He opened the front door, slammed it and yelled, 'I'm home,' and pulled me up the stairs with his finger on his lips.

His bedroom was on the top floor. It was just a shade larger than the locked rooms on 19s. We sat on his bed under the window and played Scrabble, or was it ludo — I can't remember which. We chatted and laughed. Suddenly the door was flung open and there was a scream. I could hear noises like heavy stomping on the stairs. Graham grabbed my hand and we fled down the stairs, bumping into an old man on his way up.

I was breathless and confused when we finally came to rest on a bench a little way from Graham's house.

'See what I mean, she's mad.'

I winced at the word 'mad'.

He went on to say that he wasn't allowed to have friends, especially girlfriends. He walked me home that night and kissed me good-night for the first time — and we'd been going out for six weeks.

I wanted to go home for good. I didn't want to spend my weeks in Connolly. Besides, Innesy kept picking on me and saying that I should be paying towards my keep. She said £3 would be appropriate.

'Dr Morrish, how can I pay £3? I'll have nothing left after I've paid my fares and the money I need to get home at weekends. I won't pay.'

He sat and looked at me.

'Anyway I want to go home for good. Mum says I can,' I lied.

I went home that weekend intending never to go back to St Bernard's. By the time Mum realized I wasn't going back it was too late. Because I'd lied, things didn't get off to a good start. I couldn't get up in the mornings, or rather I wouldn't. Mother's constant calling never did any good. It annoyed me so much that I put my head under the covers until eventually she went out shopping. Needless to say, owing to my persistent lateness I was fired. Because I was unemployed and at home under Mother's feet, things went from bad to worse.

One day I was sitting on the doorstep drinking a cup of tea, feeling bored and nagged at — Graham wasn't coming over either — when I saw David, the boy next door, going down the path. I followed him. He said something to annoy me, so I threw the tea over him. He chased me. I jumped over the little garden fence and ran towards the front door, believing it to be open. My left arm went through the glass middle section, up to my shoulder. I screamed.

'Now you're for it, my girl,' Mother shouted.

I went into the kitchen, and feeling something wet on my lip I looked into the mirror. 'I'll be scarred for life. I'm bleeding to death.'

'Never mind that, Shue, look at your arm.' Mother was wrapping towels round my wrist and shoulder. Someone rang for an ambulance. They took me to Harrow Hospital. When the doctor in Casualty saw the state of my arm, he asked if it had been a suicide attempt.

I couldn't get a job now with my arm all bandaged up. The doctor said it would be like that for at least six weeks. I couldn't get the dole, so I had to go on the sick.

14

TIM

Graham and I weren't getting along since I'd been out of work and my arm was bandaged. I was sleeping late every morning, and when I did get up I either moped around or sat with my head in a book. On Thursdays I went and signed on the sick. Then I went on to the Labour Exchange to see if there were any jobs. The woman in charge suggested I should register myself as a disabled person as it would be easier to find work, since firms had to employ a few registered disabled people. I refused. I felt being touched was handicap enough without it being on paper.

She had meant for me to register my diabetes as the handicap.

One day my mother visited the hospital for a check-up, and Graham popped in unexpectedly. I made him a drink. He asked me if I wanted to be manipulated. I giggled. We went to bed, and after I wondered where the WOW feeling was. From start to finish it had taken Graham two and a half minutes. I didn't see the point. I was 16 and eight months. That had been my first full experience with a man. I didn't bother for a long time after.

A few days later I had to visit Dr Morrish on Connolly. Before I left, Mum said she'd be out when I got back so would I bring in fish and chips. When I got off the train I forgot, and was half-way down Long Drive before I remembered. Cursing, I ran back, and then had to wait ages for my order. When I got home Mum told me off for being late for dinner. She'd got in earlier than she'd expected and had forgotten what she'd said.

I felt miserable that night. When Mum went out, I went to

the kitchen cupboard and emptied my pills on to the table. I can't recall how many there were. I had been taking Epanutin and Ospolot for a couple of years. I scooped them all off the table and taking a cup of water poured them down my throat. Then I sat on the sofa and read for a while.

Mum came in about 10.30 p.m. She and Mrs Hill tried to wake me but couldn't. Mum thought I was hypo and went into the kitchen for sugar water. She saw the empty pill bottles and told Mrs Hill to ring for an ambulance. I could feel Mum slapping my face. They took me to Harrow Hospital and pumped my stomach. Apparently I kicked up a fuss, shouting and screaming. They kept me overnight for observation. In the morning they transferred me to St Bernard's.

I was surprised when I was admitted to Connolly. Sister Williams was on duty and greeted me cordially. I was put back in the same bed in the right-hand dormitory. Josie and Janet were still there. Josie shook her head when she saw me, saying, 'She should be in 19s.'

'Arseholes.'

My mum wasn't on the phone so I rang Mrs Hill and she fetched Mum.

'Mum, I'm sorry I was naughty.'

'Shue, you're a silly girl.'

'It was your fault, Mum. You told me to buy the fish and chips.'

'Yes, Shue, I got home earlier than I thought and forgot.'

The pips went. I didn't have any more money. When the line went dead I waited a few minutes before I hung up.

Dr Morrish came on the ward that evening. I know he told me off but I can't recall exactly what he said. Events are a bit hazy at this time. I believe I spent about four months on Connolly before I went home again.

I was in no particular hurry to go home.

There was a boy called Steven aged about 19. He was nice-looking and I fancied him. He was a drug addict trying to rehabilitate. I tried to get him to chat but he wouldn't. He sat nodding his head even when I wasn't talking. I made it hard for him to resist me. But he did. He was homosexual. Well, I thought, I can't win them all.

Josie's friend Janet was 26 years old. She was six feet tall, with small hands and feet. Her hair was fair, cut in a page-boy style. Her face was long and pinched. She had a gold bracelet with lots of charms which made it really heavy. She would stand for hours ironing. She even ironed her tights. She wrote out Bobby Goldsboro's 'Honey' for me. I played that record continuously until Josie smashed it, saying, 'Fucking kid drives me mad.'

Dawn was 22. I hated her on sight. She was one of those people who had others flocking around her. She would sit like a queen on her throne and suffer these common people. She called her fanny her 'murk'.

Connolly started therapy sessions. Everyone talked about themselves in front of each other and the doctor asked someone to comment. Josie always took me to pieces.

During therapy one time I said to Josie, 'Do you know what I hate about you? You never offer me tea when you make it.'

'Kids don't need tea. If you want something you should get it yourself.'

Dr Morrish interjected and asked why I should get my own when she was going round with it anyway.

'I'm not waiting on her hand and foot. I'm old enough to be her mother.'

'Josie, when I make the tea I always offer you a cup.'

'But I don't want it, do I?'

'That's only because I made it.'

Doreen interrupted with another matter. Even after that, Josie never offered me a cup of tea while I was there.

Christine loved Dr Morrish almost as much as I did. She was about 34 (she wouldn't tell me her age). She was short and plump, with an oval face surrounded by dark curls. She giggled all the time. When Dr Morrish came on the ward she'd hurry down the corridor, squealing, 'He's here.' She would flop into an armchair, hugging her knees to her chest, with her eyes closed and a beam on her face. If Dr Morrish didn't see her one day she'd be inconsolable and spend the rest of the day in bed.

Timothy was a new doctor who resembled Dr Morrish in the way he looked. He was 32; I was nearly 17. It all began when he sat in on a therapy session on Connolly. He was kind and attentive when he spoke to me. He suggested we go for a walk on his day off. I couldn't see any harm.

He picked me up outside Connolly. He had a guitar with him. We walked and finally settled down in a field at the back of St Bernard's. He played 'Apache' by the Shadows. It was lovely. When he'd finished he pulled me down on the grass and kissed me. He took my breath away. I had to come up for air.

Tim had been courting me for two weeks when he used his pass key to come into Connolly one night. He gently awakened me and told me to slip into my clothes and come for a walk. He took me to his room in the doctors' quarters. He placed his mattress on the floor and began to undress me. He said he loved me. He was going to take me away from St Bernard's, make love to me and give me his babies. His words became erotic and I was ready for him. He was gentle and caring with his kisses and caresses. I never thought a man from the outside world would ever want me. I was overwhelmed by his tenderness and fell in love.

When he'd taken me back to my bed and kissed me good-night, he went over to Ellis Ward and told Staff Nurse Cooper that he'd put Miss Read back to bed. Staff Nurse Cooper asked where I'd been. He told her he'd taken me to his room and we'd made love.

Next morning Dr Morrish wanted to see me.

'Do you want to tell me what happened last night, Sue?'

'Nothing.'

'Sue, I heard different.'

'What you heard?'

'Staff Nurse Cooper says you were in Tim's bed.'

'I bet you wish it was yours,' I shouted at him.

'When he'd put you back to bed, he went and told Staff Nurse what he'd been doing.'

'He's a lying bastard. It's wishful thinking.'

Dr Morrish sat there waiting for me to explain.

'I'm discharging myself from this shit-hole. Even the doctors are fucking perverts.'

'Sue calm down. No one's blaming you. You're here for your own care and protection.'

'Crap. I've got to be mad to stop here. Tim says it's called making love.' I looked away from Dr Morrish and began to cry.

'Sue, I have to know what happened. Not only your version but Tim's too.'

'I'd rather make love with Tim than be fucked by Pauline.'

Dr Morrish explained that Tim wouldn't be able to practise there as a doctor until after the inquiry.

That afternoon Tim came for me with his guitar. While he played 'Apache' I leant my head on his shoulder and cried softly. He held me close, kissing away my tears. He asked me to marry him because he wanted to look after me. He started to make love. I tensed, saying, 'No, we mustn't. We're in enough trouble already.'

'Darling, I don't care. I'll tell the world I've made love to you.'

I knew doctors didn't make love to their patients. He was risking his career. Tim asked me why I was in St Bernard's. I told him what I could. He asked if he could meet my mother. I rang Mum to ask if I could bring him home. She was appalled at his cheek. I took him home anyway.

Tim asked Mum if she minded us continuing our relationship. He said, 'I feel it is doing Susan good.'

'You mean it's doing you good, Dr Francis.'

Mr Fletcher, Mum's Methodist minister, met Tim on a number of occasions. I'm not sure why.

One afternoon Tim didn't turn up for our walk. I waited ages, then went to look for him. I went to the field where we'd sat. I went to his room and hammered on the door. When I got back to Connolly I flung myself on the bed and howled with rage. He'd gone. I'd known he would sooner or later. Now the time had come I wasn't ready. I hadn't even kissed him goodbye.

Dr Morrish said, 'It's for the best, Sue.'

I concluded that these people always knew best. They hurt me for the best. They locked me up for the best. They took Tim away for the best. Whose best? Not mine. A nutter doesn't have a best. A nutter doesn't know the difference.

After I'd calmed down a little and howled out my rage I became frightened. I thought I'd be moved back to 18s. But as the days passed and I was still on Connolly I began to relax.

'I want to go home, Dr Morrish.'

'What does Mother say about that?'

'Who cares? I'm going home.'

'Have you got a job?'

'No problem. I'll go out tomorrow and get one.'

Dr Morrish nodded.

Once again I caught the bus opposite the gates into Greenford. I went into every shop, asking for work. After about eight refusals I was going to give up. I thought, I'll try the Curtis shoe shop before giving up. The girl asked me to wait and disappeared into the back of the shop. I sat on a chair by the door as it was a warm day. The girl reappeared with a man. He introduced himself as the manager. I can't recall his name. He asked me a few questions and said I could start the next day, which was a Saturday. I felt too depressed to rush back to Connolly squealing, 'I've got a job'.

That evening I said to Dr Morrish, 'I've got a job. Now can I go home?'

'Mmm, let's wait a week and see how you get on.'

'For Christ's sake, I want to go home.'

'Let's wait a week, Sue.' He spoke in a tone that meant I didn't have any alternative but to wait the week.

The week carried on into a month, then six weeks. It was easy for me to get to work from St Bernard's. The staff didn't allow me to laze in bed in the mornings. I had to be up and out. I knew deep down that if I went home it wouldn't be easy for me to get to work, especially from the transport point of view. I wouldn't have got up in the mornings either. It would not have been long before I was in the same situation as before.

The job was all right. I wasn't too keen on people's smelly feet. The other girls were friendly enough and a little older than me. One day I was helping a woman to decide which pair of shoes she wanted. I had shown her seven pairs and she was still umming and ahing when I looked out of the window. I saw a man watching me. A little later, when the shop was full of customers, the man walked in and in front of everyone he asked me if I'd go out with him that night.

'No,' I said, disappearing into the back of the shop. When I came out a few minutes later he'd gone.

The same evening I was making my way to the bus stop when he appeared out of nowhere. Without any preamble he said, 'We'll have a meal and go to the pictures.'

He wasn't anything special to look at, but he was cheeky so I said, 'Why not?'

His name was Billy. He was short and plump, with a round face and large brown eyes. His hair was jet black and there was just the hint of a moustache. He was Irish. I found his accent fascinating.

We had a good evening together. He asked me to his place for a coffee. He lived in Greenford with his brother, his sister-in-law and their children. He took me in by the back door, which led straight into the kitchen. He filled the kettle and put it on the stove, then led me into the living-room. 'This is Sue.'

'Hello there,' they said together.

Billy went back to the kitchen when the kettle started to whistle. His brother put his hand on my knee. I tensed, and looking at his wife I thought, Oh my God.

The wife stood up, saying, 'If you want to go upstairs with them I don't mind.'

Billy led me upstairs; his brother followed. The brother undid the buttons on my blouse and unzipped my skirt. Billy had already undressed and was standing by the bed naked. I didn't wear a bra in those days, so I was left in my knickers watching the brother undress. I remember feeling powerless yet excited. They began caressing me and once I started to relax I caressed them too. I lost track of time but eventually Billy entered me while his brother and sister-in-law made love together.

I didn't enjoy the sex with Billy. But I did enjoy the games we'd played. I went out with him for a fortnight. I tried to initiate the bed scene each time I went to the house, but to no avail. They never attempted anything like that with me again, in fact Billy didn't have any physical contact with me except for a good-night kiss.

When Billy and I split up I didn't see any point in working at the shoe shop. I gave in my notice.

15

DIFFICULTIES

Since Tim had left I'd become more and more depressed. Now I was out of work. I went to see Dr Morrish. 'I'm going home. You can't fucking stop me.'

'All right Sue, go home.'

'I fucking will.'

I slammed out of his office, threw my things into a carrier bag and stormed out of Connolly. 'No slamming doors on my ward,' Innesy said as I passed her in the corridor.

'Stupid prat.'

I arrived on Mum's doorstep in a foul mood. She asked me what I wanted. 'I'm home,' I said, pushing past her and going into the kitchen.

'But Shue, do the doctors know? You can't just turn up, disrupting the whole household.'

I went upstairs to put my things away. As my bed wasn't made up I fetched sheets and blankets from the airing cupboard.

'Have you got a job, Shue? You have to pay your way, you do.'

I didn't answer. She knew I didn't have a job. She went into Mrs Hill's and rang Connolly.

'Dr Morrish said you were in a foul mood and he couldn't stop you. Shue, it won't work here if you're not working.'

'But why, Mum? I'll get the dole. I can't stay there any more.'

'You're not my only child, Shue. What about the others?'

'Fuck them. What about me for a change? I'm home and I'm stopping.'

Mother sat down, took off her glasses and put her head in

her hands. She sighed deeply and resigned herself to my being home.

Next day I went to the Labour Exchange. There was a post at Alkan Ltd, not far from Mother's house. I applied for the job, and got it. I would be trained as a filing clerk and relief telephonist. It was an interesting job and the wages were reasonable.

I didn't have a boyfriend. There wasn't much to do in the evenings. Some nights I went to the youth club at the church around the corner. I was getting more depressed. Mother and I still didn't get along. Pauline and I fought like cat and dog. Life at home was worse than in St Bernard's.

At every opportunity I went back to St Bernard's on some pretext or other. On Thursdays I went to the social. After one such visit to the social I brought Angela home with me.

Angela was tall and angular. She had a sweet pretty face with fair hair that hung down in ringlets. I had known her from the unit in Hanwell. Angela's mother had been in 19s with me. She was a reserved woman with eight children, Angela being the eldest. When her mother had become ill and was admitted to St Bernard's, Angela had taken over looking after the younger ones, until she too ended up in 18s, by which time I'd been moved to Connolly.

Angela was slow in her movements. If you asked her a question she thought awhile before answering. On the way home with me she told me she was the children's mother and her father's wife, now that her mother wasn't around. I didn't know what she meant. I knew the children had been taken into care when Angela had become an inmate. She explained that her father and she were like man and wife; they slept together. I was shocked.

Mum was nervous when I brought Angela home, especially when she began talking about suicide. Angela went into the toilet before we went up to bed. I had never seen my mum move so fast. She took every pill bottle, every knife and even the Domestos to bed with her. 'Just in case, Shue. We don't want a dead body on our hands now, do we?'

Angela left in the morning. I saw her occasionally at the

socials, but she didn't talk to me again except for 'hello' and 'goodbye'.

One morning I got up to go to work. When I was nearly there I changed my mind on an impulse and went to St Bernard's instead. I arrived early in the morning. I knew Dr Morrish wouldn't be there until the evening. Christine kept saying, 'Ooh, you lucky thing, making love with Tim.'

'I thought you loved Dr Morrish.'

'Oh I do. Tim's the next best thing. Ooh, what was it like?'

I described it in exaggerated detail. Christine was a silly woman who believed everything everyone said.

Josie was hateful to me and I belted her in the mouth. She threw herself into a chair, screaming. Innesy came running, puffing with exertion. She took in the scene immediately. I was still standing over Josie, who had her hands covering her head, still screaming full force. When I saw Innesy, in defence I said, 'She called me a slut.'

'I don't care what she called you. I won't have violence on my ward.'

'Stop her screaming or I'll fucking belt her again.'

'Come on Josie, stop that noise now. Let's go to the office and sort this out.' Innesy had her arm round Josie's shoulder and was leading her out of the living area. She turned to me as she reached the door and said, 'As for you, get out of my ward, or else.'

'No, I'm here to see Dr Morrish and I ain't going nowhere till I've seen him.'

When Dr Morrish arrived, Innesy told him what had happened and Josie was in his office for ages. I sat outside his office seething. I even banged on the door, shouting, 'Hurry up.'

When Josie finally left and I did see Dr Morrish he was cross. 'What a stupid thing to do. Hitting her was stupid.'

'She called me a slut. Me a slut. She's more of a slut with all that crap on her face and that lousy wig.'

'That doesn't mean you can hit her.'

'She's not pushing me around, the fucking old cow'

'Sue, you shouldn't be here anyway. You're spending too

much time here. You should be at work.'

'Give me a prescription and I'll go. I'm not coming back either. I know when I'm not wanted.'

He wrote out the prescription and said, 'Goodbye, Sue.'

'Fuck off.'

I fumed all the way home. 'Everyone hates me, even Dr Morrish. What's the point?' I got off the train and changed the prescription before I went home. The chemist gave me a bottle of 50 Epanutin, 50 Ospolot and 50 Valium.

I banged on the front door without a break until Mum opened it. 'All right Shue, what's the matter with you? Banging like that.'

'Get out of my way.' I elbowed my way past her. After I'd eaten my dinner I sat and watched TV. I must have dozed off. When I awoke there was no one around. I wandered through the house and ended up sitting at the kitchen table. I thought to myself, If I was dead I'd be able to look down and listen to what people really thought of me. Mother would be sitting there on a Saturday evening saying, 'Well at least I won't be afraid to open the front door any more in case it's Susan.' That's it then, I decided. I would kill myself and it would serve them right for hating me so much.

On the table were the three bottles of pills. Without thinking further I went to the sink, filled a mug with water and emptied some of the pills from each bottle into the palm of my hand. I put them into my mouth in two goes, followed by the water. Then I went into the living-room and lay on the sofa.

About 11 p.m. Mother came in and tried to rouse me. I staggered up and wet myself on the living-room carpet. She knew what I'd done straight away and told Pam to ring for an ambulance. Mum told me afterwards that I kept repeating 'I won't be sick' in parrot fashion. The ambulance took me to Mount Vernon. There they pumped my stomach for the second time. It wasn't a nice experience. Mother said I was screaming that I would murder her if she came near me.

I remember waking up in the main ward with screens pulled around my bed. I got out of bed and peeped round the

curtains to see what was going on. I was grabbed by two
nurses, dragged back on the bed and held there, while they
yelled for someone to call the doctor. It was a lady doctor. She
told the nurses to leave but to stay close by. 'Miss Read, I'm
going to administer your insulin and then you can have
breakfast.'

'I do my own insulin.'

She called the nurses. They held me while she gave me a
dose of paraldehyde. While unconscious from the effects of
paraldehyde I was transferred to St Bernard's.

I awoke on Conway (which was for admissions), being
pulled and slapped by a young doctor. I was lying naked
except for my knickers on a narrow couch in a consulting-
room. The doctor had obviously got a report from Mount
Vernon. He scowled at me, saying, 'If it wasn't for Dr Morrish
you'd be on 18s in the PR. You'd better be careful with me
because I'll not hesitate dumping you back there.'

'Go away.'

'You've caused everyone a great deal of trouble, not to
mention your poor mother.'

'Don't then.'

Later I was moved to Connolly. They put me in the bed by
the door, still in the right-hand dormitory. Willie came down
and told me to put on my dressing-gown as Dr Morrish
wanted to see me. He was so kind to me. I felt awful for
letting him down. He asked me what had happened before I
went into Mount Vernon. I told him how depressed I felt.
How pointless everything seemed. And how even though I
didn't want to be in St Bernard's I was finding it so difficult to
cope outside. I couldn't seem to do anything right.

I'm not sure how long I stayed in Connolly this time. I know I
had my 16th birthday there.

Connolly had organized a trip to London to see Agatha
Christie's *The Mousetrap*. The coach was outside Connolly
waiting to take everyone to the theatre. I was standing with
Willie, waving goodbye. Dr Morrish appeared and asked me
why I wasn't going with them. I told him I didn't have any

money. He put his hand in his pocket and gave me the £3 needed. The rest of the ward weren't pleased I was going. Josie muttered, 'Wherever she goes there's trouble.' I sat next to Christine. She prattled on about Tim until I told her to shut up.

Another time I went with Connolly to Greenwich to see the Cutty Sark.

I had a few jobs while I was there this time. One of them was cleaning cars in a garage in Ealing. The garage was on the corner of a side-road. Every day this old lady passed me while I was polishing the cars on the forecourt. 'Morning, dear,' she'd say, smiling.

'Morning, missus.'

She passed one day while I was eating my lunch. She noticed I was drinking my tea black. 'Do you like your tea black, my dear?'

'No, but I haven't any milk.'

'If you like you can have your lunch at my house. I have plenty of milk, dearie.'

'Thank you.'

'Well, come along. Follow me, dear.'

I did. She lived three doors up on the right-hand side of the road. She fumbled in her bag for the door keys; I stepped into the dreary hallway. The house smelt musty — the sort of smell you get when you brush a carpet. The furniture was of dark wood and old. I looked down; there were four black cats mewing round my ankles. I cringed. I didn't like cats.

The kitchen was more of a scullery. It looked like my Nanny's. 'Here's the milk, dear.' She pointed to the draining-board. There was a washing-up bowl half-filled with water. A milk bottle three-quarters full was standing in the water.

'Don't you have a fridge, missus?'

'Oh no, dear, I don't go for all these new ideas.' She made me a cup of tea. 'We'll make ourselves comfortable in here, dear.'

I followed her into the living-room. There were lumps of sour milk floating on top of my tea. She chatted away, telling me about her mum and dad. She said how crowded it had got in Ealing. Nearly everything she said was preceded by 'I remember when'.

In the house opposite the old lady's lived two brothers. They were in their late sixties. The lady told me one day they were looking for a lodger. She took me over and introduced me to them. They looked like twins to me. I did not know it at the time but they lived in a maisonette. The stairs were in front of the door. They led the way and we turned left at the top. They showed me the room. I could only open the door about 12 inches, and once I'd squeezed in I could only take three steps. The room was cram-packed with old chairs, large boxes and rolls of carpet. There was a thick layer of dust over everything. They said if I cleaned the room I could live there rent-free. It looked a daunting task but I thought, Why not? It's better than St Bernard's and it will keep me busy for a while.

'I've got somewhere to lie and it's for free. I'll be leaving in a week or two,' I told Dr Morrish.

'Where?'

'Near where I work.'

'Who's it with?'

'Two men, they're brothers.'

'I don't think that's wise, Sue, especially if it's rent-free.'

'But they're old. I'm going to clean the room; that's why it's free. I described the state of the room.

He nodded. 'Offer them something for rent, Sue.'

'They insisted they didn't want anything.'

'Just £1, Sue, offer them something.'

'All right, all right.' I sighed loudly.

I did as Dr Morrish had suggested. They wouldn't accept anything. When I reported back to Dr Morrish he said, 'In that case I can't allow you to live there.'

'Oh but I want to.'

'No,' he said, shaking his head.

'You hate me, you bastard. You want me to stay here for ever and ever.' I smashed the door of his office up against the wall several times before I stamped off to the dormitory.

I didn't bother to go to work any more.

Things started getting bad again. I became more depressed than usual. When I wasn't yelling about something I would slope off for hours on end. A few times I went over to the bus station opposite the gates. I didn't have anywhere to go, so I sat in the busmen's canteen drinking tea and eating dough-nuts. I got lots of offers for dates, but declined.

One day I walked into Hanwell. I was sitting by a pond in the park, when a man approached me. 'You'd make a good model,' he said, adding, 'being so skinny.'

'Oh yeah.'

He showed me a magazine pointing out how skinny the models were. 'See, they're all skinny, just like you.'

I didn't say anything. I sat leafing through the magazine.

'Ring this number and ask for an appointment,' he said, handing me a thin slip of paper with a number on it. He walked away.

I rang the number and arranged an appointment in two days. The agency was in Maida Vale. I was full of nerves when I arrived. On the door was a notice saying not to enter until the blinds were up. I glanced at my watch and saw I still had six minutes to go before my appointment. I looked in the window at pictures of models; they were all slim and made up.

The blind was up when I next looked. I went in. A girl sitting at the desk said, 'Yes, can I help you?'

'I've got an appointment for 11.15.'

'Wait here,' she said, disappearing through another door. The reception was bare except for her desk. The girl reappeared, saying, 'This way.' She led me into another room. It was larger than reception. In one corner was a wooden chair with a high back; in the other corner was a tripod with a camera mounted on it.

There was a man and a woman. The man was short with a huge backside. I couldn't see much of his face as he was wearing huge horn-rimmed glasses. His hair was carrot-coloured and tied in a pony-tail. The woman wore the same glasses. Her teeth were horsy and she swallowed deeply after every few words. 'Take all your clothes off,' she said.

'All of them?'

'Yes, everything. Leave them on that chair,' she said, pointing to the chair in the corner. I took off my clothes, leaving them neatly on the chair, and stood naked. She walked towards me, saying, 'Shame about your hair. Good bone structure. Kneel down.' I knelt down. 'Put your hands on your hips.'

The man took two pictures. The woman went to the door and called something I couldn't hear. The girl from reception came in with a valise case.

'Make her up and cover those tattoos,' she told the girl.

The girl made up my face, covered the tattoos and left the room.

'Kneel down again. Put both hands behind your head.' I did. She came over and twiddled my nipples. 'That's better,' she said, smiling at me.

The man took a number of pictures. They were all nude, but not distasteful.

Shaking her head and waving her hands, the woman said, 'That's enough for now, I'll ring you in a few days.' She and the man left the room. I put my clothes on and went into the reception area.

The girl said, 'They're just to see if you're photogenic.'

'Oh,' I muttered as I left.

I'd already decided I'd had enough of St Bernard's and would go home again as soon as I had a job. Now I thought I had one. The next day I packed my things and went home to Mother. She wasn't pleased, but when I told her I had a job she didn't seem so agitated.

I had given the agency Mrs Hill's phone number. Two days after I went home they rang, and I went to see them. This time the woman was the same, but there was a different man. He was bald and thin. His trousers were baggy and he smelt of garlic.

'Clothes off,' said the woman. I began to undress. 'Put them on the floor, we'll need the chair.' I put my clothes on the floor, making sure it was a clean spot. 'Straddle the chair.'

'No, I'd rather not.'

She stood up, removing her clothes. I was astounded. She

113

walked up behind me, and putting her hands on my hips she pressed herself up against my bottom. I shrugged her off, put my clothes on and left.

As I waited for my train I said aloud, 'There goes another job.'

16

STEVE

I'd had 17 jobs in the three months I'd been home. I'd even been unemployed for a couple of weeks between jobs. Once I had three jobs in one day. I started at Woolworth's in Ruislip Manor in the morning. I didn't like it, so I left at lunchtime. I got a job at Bunce's sweet shop at 12.30 p.m. The lady there wasn't nice, so I left and started work at Tesco's at 4 p.m. There were two Tesco supermarkets in Ruislip Manor, one at each end of the High Street.

I worked at Tesco's for about eight weeks. I was still visiting Connolly and going to the social Thursday nights. Mother said, 'Shue, you get bored too quickly. What you need is a hobby.' I tried knitting. I was hopeless. I soon got bored and gave it up. I read lots of books, mostly about Jewish concentration camps. I've always been interested in the atrocities of war.

I began going to the Northcote Arms in Southall with Pamela and her friend Joyce. It was a club for greasers. The rock-and-roll music and dancing was what I needed to expel some of my energy. I started going out on dates with greasers. It was great fun riding pillion. We didn't use crash helmets then either. A fellow called Ken had a Triumph Bonneville 650. He took me to other clubs, like the Railway Hotel in Harrow. Mother thought they were undesirables and I would get into trouble.

I'd been waiting 40 minutes in the pouring rain for a bus to work at Tesco's. I was dripping wet and none too pleased when I got in. The manager said, 'Where have you been?'

'Swimming, where do you think?'

'You're 45 minutes late. You should have been here, not swimming.'

I thought, how stupid can he get. 'Don't be stupid, man, I've been waiting for the bus,' I flared, making my way to the locker room for my overall.

'How dare you speak to me like that. Collect your cards.'

'Stuff 'em.' I walked out.

I arrived home wet, furious and unemployed. Mum and Mrs Hill were having a cup of tea in Mum's kitchen. 'Oh no, Mrs Hill, I can't put up with her under my feet all day again.' They sat talking about me as if I wasn't there. I changed my clothes and sat in the living-room with my book.

When I got fed up with Mother's nagging and with being unemployed, I went out looking for work again. This time I got a job in the Tesco's at the other end of the High Street. My job was filling the fridges with butter and other dairy produce. The manager was an old, thin man. He was stooped, with a long nose and beady eyes. He had a lot of grey hair that kept falling down over his eyes. He would blow the hair from his eyes unsuccessfully until finally he swept it aside.

There were two young men. One was Roy, a mod with large boots and a green parka. The other was Steve — who's now my husband. I asked Roy which lunch break Steve took, and then arranged to have mine at the same time.

It was November 1970. I'd just turned 17. Decimalization was coming into effect in February 1971. Every Monday morning for an hour the shop was closed and we were trained on decimalization. I always sat next to Steve and made it obvious I fancied him. He wasn't embarrassed; he didn't seem to notice. At home-time, when Steve and Roy ran for the bus I would grab hold of Steve's coat so they didn't leave me behind. He never got cross.

Steve's job was unloading the delivery trucks and putting goods on the conveyor belt, then running upstairs to unload them. If someone wanted something in the shop they yelled up the stairs and Steve would send it down.

I smoked quite heavily then, and got Steve into the habit.

Daphne and Lil were two middle-aged women who worked on the tills. They were fond of Steve and disapproved of me.

Steve had a maroon-coloured Anglia. He hadn't passed his

test, but he drove it everywhere without L-plates. Steve never asked me out. I just tagged along. He and Roy went to a club in Ruislip Manor called the Way In. There were a few greasers, but the majority were a religious group. I asked Steve for a kiss. He didn't answer. Roy said, 'Go on, Steve, give her a kiss.' Steve pretended not to hear. Roy said he'd kiss me, and before I knew it about five greasers were lined up for a kiss, their eyes closed and lips puckered.

Why not, I thought. I said, 'OK, but only if Steve gives me one after,' amid roars of laughter. I kissed them all. I approached Steve, my heart thumping. I didn't give him a chance to protest.

He had his Anglia outside. I said, 'I'll drive.' I got in the driver's seat and turned to Steve, saying, 'Where's the ignition?'

He went pale and said, 'Get out, I'll drive.'

Roy and Steve's sister Paula were in the back seat snogging. When Steve drew up outside my house I tried to kiss him again but he wouldn't let me. As I flung the car door open to get out I shouted, 'You bleeding queer or something?'

On a Friday evening everyone worked until 8 p.m. I asked Steve if he'd come home with me for something to eat. I bought two gammon steaks in the delicatessen. When we got home Mum was on her knees washing the kitchen floor. I kicked her backside, saying to Steve, 'This is the old girl.'

'Oh Shue, I wish you wouldn't do that.'

'Get up and cook these,' I told her, putting the gammon steaks on the table.

About 10 p.m. Steve said he had to go. I didn't want him to and tried to stop him. When he still insisted on leaving I took a steak knife and cut a chunk of his hair. I still have the hair; it's in the shape of an S.

He did leave. Next day I was late getting into work. Steve was refilling the soft-drinks shelf just inside the door. When he saw me he stepped out in front of me and said, 'Sue, I . . .'

I didn't give him a chance to finish. I barged past him angrily, saying, 'Get out of my way.' I ran upstairs for my overall. I had had my insulin and no breakfast. By the time I'd got into work, tea break was over. Lunchtime arrived and I felt dizzy.

I don't remember anything else.

Steve told me after that he and Roy went to the baker's to get their rolls for lunch. They saw a crowd of people outside the baker's. Roy said, 'Hey Steve look, it's Sue.'

There was a man kneeling beside me, putting a spoon between my teeth. The man was the chemist from over the road. He asked if anyone knew me. Steve said, 'That's my girl.' He told the chemist I was diabetic. I was taken to Mount Vernon again.

Steve told me after that he and the under-manager, Bob Arnold, went to Mount Vernon to see if they could bring me back. When Steve told the nurse that I was his girlfriend she said, 'My advice to you is to wash your hands of her.' They wouldn't allow them to see me.

When I woke up I was back in St Bernard's. Mother told me later what had happened. A man from Mount Vernon had knocked on Mum's door and said I'd been found on the street unconscious and raving. When the authorities had reluctantly admitted me to Mount Vernon my behaviour had left a lot to be desired.

They asked Mother to sign a paper to readmit me to St Bernard's or they would put me on a section by going through the courts. Mum signed and I went back to St Bernard's.

Luckily I went to Connolly. Dr Morrish was furious with the authorities. He thought they shouldn't have sent me back for being hypo; they should have given me sugar and a stern lecture. He told me off for my irresponsibility. He said that if I agreed to stay for a week he'd ignore the section.

I was more concerned with losing Steve. I rang him that evening. I was surprised to be told it was Sunday. Mount Vernon had given me paraldehyde again and I'd been asleep for 24 hours. I asked Steve if he'd come and see me. He turned up around 8.30 p.m.

Steve was never a great talker. We walked through the grounds, me talking and Steve listening. I knew I didn't have any claims on Steve. I told him this and said I didn't want to lose him. When he left he kissed me goodbye without any prompting from me. The next time he came he brought his sister Paula with him. She brought me some cigarettes.

I stayed the week. Steve visited as often as he could. When the week was up I went home and back to Tesco's. A few weeks later I was offered a job at London Bankside in South Ruislip. I persuaded Steve to leave Tesco's and work with me. Tesco's were sorry to lose him and offered a £1 rise if he stayed.

I told Mum I was leaving Tesco's.

'Shue, I'm not putting up with it. You either work or you find somewhere else to live, you do.'

'Look Mum, I'm going to work at London Bankside up the road so shut your nagging.'

'What will you be doing there?'

'I'm not sure yet.' I shrugged my shoulders.

'Probably making toilet-rolls,' Mum said seriously. She thought I'd said London Backside. We've often laughed about that.

Steve and I worked there for about three months before the firm announced they were moving to Denham. We were both earning good money; it was piece-work. When they closed down I got another job straight away. It was on the same industrial estate, with a suede and leather firm called Dickens. There was a mountain of suede or leather. My job was to sort out and put into piles the sleeves, backs, collars etc. At Christmas I made belts at home for an extra bonus. Steve meanwhile had started at Dixons photographic in Acton. He was in the warehouse loading the bays.

Steve's brother John was travelling with his father in the cab of an articulated lorry carrying Lucozade. The lorry jack-knifed and John got hurt. I recall that battery acid was dripping on to John's leg so his dad poured Lucozade over his leg. John went to a hospital in Gloucester, and when Steve's family went to visit him one Sunday, Steve got into his house through the toilet window. We sat and watched TV for a while. I had known Steve for nearly 10 months and in all that time he'd only ever kissed me. That Sunday we went to bed together and I cried.

Steve passed his driving test and changed his Anglia for a Mini. I spent Christmas at Steve's. It was the best Christmas I'd ever had. There was a crowd, since there were 10 children in the family, and with boyfriends and girlfriends it was a real party to me.

I left Dickens and had a short period of unemployment. Then I worked at a small publishing firm in North Acton. I left after a couple of weeks. I started work at Kodak. After I'd left there I had a few jobs waitressing in various hotels. One was the Rayners Hotel in Rayners Lane. I was employed to prepare the sandwiches and lunchtime food they served in the bars. I had to live in, which suited me fine as Mother and I were quarrelling every day now.

I had to be up at 6 a.m. An old man banged on my bedroom door each morning at 5.45 a.m. I never saw him, but I knew he was old because his voice crackled. The manager's wife was in her middle fifties. She had a large head on a long neck. Her eyes were set wide apart; the lids drooped and fluttered as if she was going to fall asleep any minute. She showed me what to do every morning; then she'd say, 'Stand back,' and she'd do it herself. 'You mash the potatoes like this,' and she'd mash the potatoes. She had a thin grating voice which infuriated me. The once that I did ask if I could make the sandwiches she said, 'Yes, girl, this is how it's done,' and did it herself. I was there about three weeks and I don't remember lifting a finger.

On one of my weekends off Steve and I got engaged. He bought me a heart-shaped engagement ring. Our families went out for a meal to a restaurant in Ealing called Never on a Sunday. It was my 18th birthday the following day, so we celebrated both.

The manager's wife told her husband I was lazy and she had to do all my work as well as her own. I told the manager what had been happening when he gave me my cards. He said, 'I know, she's always been like that.'

My next job was at the Air Force base in Northolt. Again I

lived in. When I'd been sacked from the Rayners and moved home again, Mother had been emphatic that I wouldn't be stopping. So when I got a job in the kitchens at the RAF base, I concocted a story about Mother having died and my being homeless. The lady in charge was sympathetic and found me a room.

Even though I was engaged to Steve, I developed an awful crush on an airman called Rocky. He had blond hair and blue eyes. There was a jagged scar on his right cheek from under his eye to his jaw. He was really thin, with enormous feet. Everyone joked about Rocky's feet.

He knew I fancied him. He asked me back to his billet one night. I accepted. Without any preliminaries he dropped his trousers and threw me on his bed. I was petrified; I thought he was going to rape me. Stalling for time, I suggested we took things a bit slower. He was all for that and lay back on the bed with a smirk on his face.

When I saw it my eyes nearly popped out of my head. I thought, no way, that'll kill me. I ran out of his room. Rocky never spoke to me again. I tried not to make it so obvious I fancied a bloke after that, or to go anywhere alone with them.

Steve often stopped the night with me when Eileen wasn't there. Eileen and I were good friends and shared the same room. She was tall and dark, about 30 years old. When I asked her where she lived or anything about her family she changed the subject.

We worked opposite shifts. One afternoon I came off my early-morning shift to find our room had been ransacked. I'd had a beautiful white gold bracelet wrist-watch and about £70 in cash in my small travelling-case. Eileen had made it look like someone had entered the room through the window. The police said it was her. She was known to them. They said the burglary had her hallmarks.

It wasn't so much the stealing my things that upset me, it was the fact that I thought she was my friend. I was so hurt that night I went out and got drunk on vodka and lime. I threw myself into bed and fell asleep. I awoke with severe stomach-ache and rushed to the hand-basin vomiting.

Maureen the cleaner was outside in the hall. She heard me vomiting and knocked on the door. The camp nurse came over. Maureen lived in the same street as Mother. She told the nurse I was diabetic. The nurse rang for an ambulance. This time they took me to Northwick Park Hospital because Mount Vernon refused to take me.

I'd been neglecting my diabetes. Sometimes I hadn't even bothered to inject my insulin. Hyperglycemia means the blood sugar is too high. If untreated the patient will eventually go into a coma. This time I was hyper. Maureen had informed Mum and she turned up at Northwick Park.

I kept getting out of bed and drinking water straight from the tap. Mother said, 'She's drinking the water.'

The nurse replied, 'Don't concern yourself, Mrs Read, she'll only vomit.'

I drank the water and vomited. The doctors arrived and put a drip in my arm.

'Now Shue, you behave yourself here and you won't end up back in St Bernard's, you won't.'

Mother rang the air-base to ask if they'd keep my job open. The lady asked if she was sure she was my mother. Mother assured her she was unfortunately. Mother was livid when the lady told her she was supposed to be dead.

'Shue, that's the wickedest thing you've ever said.'

'Oh, it was only a joke.'

'You think that's funny, do you? Shue, you've got a sick sense of humour.'

I was discharged from Northwick Park and went back to work at the air-base. Things weren't the same. Every day the lady asked if I'd done my injection. She fussed continuously.

Steve and I went for tea at Mum's one Sunday. I was sleeping the night at Mum's, as the next day was my day off. Steve and I had an argument before he left. I followed him to the doorstep and threw my engagement ring at him. It fell somewhere in the garden and we couldn't find it. Steve was furious and went home, leaving me still looking for it. The next morning I found the ring embedded in a rose.

Steve and I made up. Everything was fine until our next

row, in Bridgewater Road. Again I threw the ring at him. It was dark. We looked for ages but couldn't find it. 'We're finished now. No engagement ring means we're not engaged.' He turned his back and walked away.

I looked a little longer, with tears streaming down my face. I went home and told Mum what had happened.

'You won't learn, will you Shue.'

'I was angry with him.'

'In the morning, put an advert in West Mead shops. You never know, someone might find it.'

'Yeah, ni-night.'

Next morning I did as Mum had suggested. A week went by and I didn't hear from Steve. I cried. When I rang his house they said he wasn't in. I gave up my job at the air-base.

Mother had been shopping and came rushing in the door, squealing, 'Mrs Jones at West Mead told me someone's found your ring.'

'What? Who? Oh Mum.' I hugged her, jumping up and down.

'Careful, Shue, careful.'

I raced all the way to West Mead. Mrs Jones gave me the address of a lady in Bridgewater Road. The lady said her little boy had found it. She made me tell her where I'd lost it to make sure it was mine. She wouldn't accept anything for herself, but I insisted she took £2 for her little boy's piggy-bank.

I didn't bother to ring Steve this time. Instead I called round his house. He came out on the doorstep, pulling the door up behind him. 'Yes?'

'I've found the ring, darling.'

'Yes?'

'Yes, I put an advert in West Mead shops. A lady handed it in.'

'Oh.' He stepped back on the doorstep.

'Steve, now we can try again. I'm sorry, darling, I was a bitch.' I put my arms round his neck and kissed his lips.

He responded. Closing the front door, he took my hand and led me to his car.

'I've missed you, darling,' I told Steve as he parked the car at Ruislip Woods.

'Yes, me too.'

I'd always been fond of children, so when I was walking through Harrow and saw a position for a children's nanny in the window of a domestic agency, I went in and applied for it.

The woman in the office was about 45 years old. Her face was like granite. Her eyes stared and she spoke without moving her lips. When she left her seat and went over to the filing cabinet, I noticed she was wearing four-inch stiletto heels. Her ankles and legs were immense. The stilettos looked hideous. She made me feel inferior. Her manner reminded me of Mrs Wharton, my tutor.

'I'll arrange for an interview, but I doubt if you'll get the position.'

'I don't see why not,' I replied innocently.

'Cleaning would be more your line. Respectable people won't take you with those.' She pointed to my hands. 'Those tattoos.'

'Snob,' I said to myself.

I had an appointment for the following day. I'd been told when I got to Moor Park train station to ring Mrs Everton and she would pick me up. Mrs Everton picked me up in a grey station-wagon with two little girls giggling in the back. I was taken to the house and shown around.

A door at the end of the garage opened into a utility room with washing-machine, tumble-drier and a double sink for the hand washing. The first floor consisted of an L-shaped kitchen with all mod. cons. To the left of the small hall was the dining-room, which was only used when there were guests. There were three bay windows with heavy brocaded drapes. The dining-table was almost as long as the room. There were five chairs on each side of the table and one at each end. I called it a 'pass-the-marmalade' table. The only other piece of furniture was a long sideboard.

There were doors at each end of the dining-room. The left-hand door opened into the den. Again there were bay windows and drapes. The furniture was brown studded hide, consisting of a three-seater settee, an armchair, a rocking chair and a matching stool. On one entire wall were shelves filled with books of every description. The other wall had a small ornate fire with a mantelpiece. As this was mainly the children's room, there was a colour TV.

The right-hand door opened into the study, which you could see from the dining-room as the wall was in glass sections. In front of the bay window stood a baby grand piano. The fireplace and mantelpiece in this room were exquisite. There was an antique bureau open with papers in disarray. On one side of the fireplace were brass instruments on hooks that were for tending a fire. On the other side was a globe that when opened was a drinks cabinet.

Further along the hall to the right was the front door. To one side was a walk-in closet. On the other side, down three steps, was a toilet. Going back, in the middle of the hall on the right were the stairs with a wooden railing. The stairs were wide. There were large pictures decorating the stair-well.

At one end of the landing was the children's pink bathroom. Opposite was Mr and Mrs Everton's bedroom. Once in their bedroom, through a door on the left were fitted wardrobes in an L-shape. In the centre of the wardrobes was a dressing table and numerous drawers. To the right behind a small alcove was a blue bathroom and shower tiled with mirrors. In the bedroom was a five-foot bed with bedside cabinets, a Queen Anne velvet chair and an antique chest of drawers. On top of the chest of drawers, covering every inch of space, there were miniature picture frames with photos of the family.

Along the landing, after a walk-in airing cupboard, was Robbie's bedroom. Around the corner was Casey and Bethy's bedroom. Doubling back, on the left was Christopher's room. On the right was a door at the bottom of a flight of stairs which led up to my quarters. It was a rosy-papered bedroom with a round bay window, a niche with shelves and a fitted cupboard. At the other end of the landing was the playroom, with every toy imaginable, a TV and a stereogram. A door in the playroom led into my green bathroom.

Mrs Everton introduced me to the housekeeper, Betty. She said they had a gardener called Jack who came twice weekly. She asked me a number of questions and said she would let me know if she found me suitable after she'd interviewed two other girls. She drove me back to Moor Park train station.

'Mum, they're really rich. The house was beautiful.'

'Do you think you've got a chance, Shue?'

'She said she's got two more girls to see. I won't get it, Mum.'

When the letter arrived saying she was sorry but the position was filled, I wasn't too disappointed as I'd already resigned myself. A week later Mrs Hill came in. 'There's a phone call for Sue. A Mrs Imberson.'

'I don't know anyone called Imberson.'

I went along to Mrs Hill's and said 'hello' into the receiver.

'Mum, Mum, I've got the job. I don't believe it.' I twirled her round.

'What job? Stop it, Shue,' she said, slapping me playfully.

'The children's nanny. I start tomorrow.' I raced upstairs to pack my case. I'd bought a suitcase the previous week from Steve's mum's mail-order club. I said, 'Bye, Mum,' and took a taxi to Moor Park.

17

GETTING MARRIED

I had dinner with the family. They told me that the girl they'd taken on last week had been homesick. They welcomed me into their family.

I awoke the next morning at 7 a.m. I dressed hurriedly and chivvied the children to wash and dress. It was bedlam at breakfast. Betty came in during the uproar, and amidst the racket said, 'When the kiddies have gone to school I'll show you what to do.' Betty became invaluable to me and a good friend too.

I soon got myself and the children into a routine. Robbie and Casey were seven and five respectively. They were at school all day. Bethy was three and at nursery in the mornings. Christopher was 14 months and stayed home with me. I had to go shopping every day, even though the freezer was stocked full with food. 'The children need plenty of fresh air and sunshine,' Mrs Everton told me.

When I'd been there a few days I told them about Steve and asked if he could call to see me in the evenings after work. They didn't mind, and made Steve welcome each time he called. Steve and I had happy days in Moor Park. Mr Everton asked Steve if he'd clean the swimming-pool. He did, and was paid £10. On a Saturday evening when Mr and Mrs Everton went out, Steve and I would pretend it was our house and they were our children. We were allowed to eat what we wanted from the freezer. Most Saturdays we had best steak and corn on the cob, until we tired of it.

I went on holiday with them to Castle Combe in Wiltshire. Another family with three children came with us. It was terrific fun looking after seven children. Whilst I was with them I visited Woburn, Longleat, Hampton Court, Blenheim Palace and many other stately homes. My mother has always said that my time with them was the making of me.

I'd been with them for 18 months when they asked if I'd like to go to Spain with them. I didn't like hot weather and was a little apprehensive. Mum and Steve persuaded me, saying, 'Shue, this is the chance of a lifetime,' and 'I'd go if they asked me.' They got me a 10-year passport. While I was in Spain, Steve was going to Herne Bay with his parents. He would have his 21st birthday while I was away.

Mrs Everton had told me not to buy sun-creams or a sun-hat until I got to Spain, as they were much cheaper and prettier there. As I'd expected, the heat was stifling. When we got there I wasn't allowed out to get a sun-hat or cream. I had to sit by the pool with the children from 8 a.m. to 7 p.m. After two days I was burnt to a crisp.

On the first day Chrissie jumped in the deep end. Mrs Everton had hysterics, screaming, 'Save him.' She lost her temper in front of everyone, shouting, 'You'd have let my baby drown.' I couldn't swim a stroke. She was a good swimmer but she expected *me* to save Chrissie.

On the fourth day I felt so ill that I asked Mrs Everton if I could stay in the hotel to give me a little respite from the sun. Again she lost her temper, saying, 'I will draw you a bath and you can soak yourself. If you want to look good you have to pay for it.' She turned the taps on in the bathroom. By the time I'd finished my chores, the bath had run over.

I soaked in the warm water, but afterwards I felt worse. 'Mrs Everton, If I can't rest tomorrow I'm going home.'

She dragged my clothes from the wardrobe and threw them on the bed. 'You're an ungrateful girl after all we've done for you. Yes, you go home. You're fired.' She went to the reception and asked for a taxi. Mr Everton gave me my wages and some extra on top. She didn't like that, and said so. He said he wasn't going to be responsible for my not having any money in a foreign country.

The taxi man was over-familiar. When he stopped at a garage for petrol I asked for a drink of water. He brought me a pitcher of water. I swallowed my pill with it, thinking, if I'm going to be raped by this greasy man I can at least make sure I don't get pregnant.

We arrived at Malaga airport at about midnight. I was astonished to see policemen with rifles and other weaponry. I hadn't noticed them on landing. I went to a departure desk and showed my ticket. From what I could gather there were no flights.

I sat on a long bench, prepared to wait. A good-looking Spaniard approached me, saying, 'You go home?'

'Yes, I go home.'

'You go my home.' He pulled me by the hand.

'No.' I tried to explain that England was my home and made noises like an aeroplane.

'Me, no speak-a de Inglis.' He tried the same approach on every woman waiting — to no avail.

I finally got a flight. There was a right carry-on when they searched my hand-luggage. They found my syringe and insulin bottles. I immediately felt a rifle in my ribs. My knees were close to buckling and my mind raced with pictures of me being locked in a smelly Spanish cell. I'm sure they thought I was a drug addict.

'Diabetic. Diabeteech,' I said frantically. They went away and came back with a long-haired man. He interpreted for me and saved the day. I was a nervous wreck when I boarded the plane.

I landed at Gatwick. After the stifling heat, the steady drizzle was lovely. I changed my pesetas to pounds. I had £28. I was so tired after the flight that I didn't fancy public transport. I took a taxi home from Gatwick. It cost me £19. Mother shook her head wearily when she opened the front door, saying, 'Oh Shue.' I paid the taxi, dropped my case in the hall and went straight to bed.

I woke up and told Mum the whole story.

'You'll have to apologize, Shue, you can't come home. They'll take you back. I'll talk to them, you'll see.'

'No way, not after the way she treated me.'

It was Steve's birthday the next day. I asked Mrs Hill if I

could ring the caravan site in Herne Bay where Steve was on holiday. He was shocked to hear from me. I wished him a happy birthday and said I would see him when he got back.

Steve came home on the Saturday but I didn't see him until the Monday evening. I'd been tidying up my bedroom. I took him upstairs. He lay on my bed with his hands behind his head. He looked at me, saying, 'I'm in love.'

'Oh darling, that's really nice of you.' I bent and kissed him.

'Not with you.' He sat up.

'What do you mean, Steve?'

He told me he'd met a girl on holiday and they were in love. I was stunned, and said, 'Don't be silly, Steve.'

'It's true. We're finished now.' He got off the bed and went downstairs.

It had all happened so fast I felt shaky. By the time I got outside, Steve was in his car and driving away. I shouted after him, 'Steve, don't be silly.' Before I'd gone to Spain we'd booked the wedding and reception for February 9th, 1974.

Mother said, 'Give him a bit of freedom, Shue, it's only a holiday fling. He'll come back, you'll see.'

I rang his house every day. If he did speak to me he was offhand. It was as if we were strangers.

Weeks went by and I lived as if in a daze. Meanwhile, I'd got a job at the West Ruislip US air-base. I'd been there a few weeks when I had a row with one of the girls. I went to Personnel and told Joyce I was leaving. 'I don't have to put up with that,' I told her.

She said, 'Wait here a minute.' She returned, saying there was a vacancy in the office and should I accept it. I did. My job was filing and adding numbers on a machine with a till-roll. The money was good and the hours were less. Also, because I knew the job in the warehouse, I got plenty of overtime on Saturdays.

I was getting along a little better with Mum. She had been sympathetic when Steve had packed me in.

An American called Don asked me if I'd have dinner with him. I'd had practically no social life since Steve and I had parted. I met Don at South Ruislip station after work on

Friday night. I was wearing my brown miniskirt and matching jacket. He whistled and said, 'Wow. Where d'ya wanna go, doll? The Plough or the West End?'

'The West End, please.'

We had dinner at the Blue Boar Inn restaurant. After the meal we went to the pictures and saw *M*A*S*H*.

Don was six feet three inches tall, with dark hair and a beard. His eyes were brown and his best feature. When he smiled it made me feel warm. He weighed about 15 stone. On the way home from the station, Don put his arm round my shoulder. We got to the end of Long Drive and I said, 'I wonder how much your arm weighs.'

'Oh, very subtle.' He withdrew his arm. He kissed me on the cheek and said, 'Good-night,' and I went indoors.

I found out that Don was married, with two children. His wife was in Sweden. He was 32 and said he was a mature student, working at the air-base to make ends meet.

'Shue, no good will come from this. He's a married man.'

'I know, I told you.'

I couldn't give him up. He talked about things that interested me. He listened to my opinions. He took me out again for my 19th birthday. At Christmas he went home for the holidays. I'd come in from work and mope around.

'I told you no good would come of this, didn't I, Shue.'

'I love him, Mum,' I wailed.

Mum was kind to me. She sat down beside me and said, 'When he comes back, Shue, don't start up with him again. Forget him, Shue.'

'I can't help it, Mum.'

I tried to be cheerful over Christmas but it was difficult. Steve came round. We went to Ruislip Woods and made love in the car. I had missed Steve's love-making and was missing Don too; I couldn't say no. After Christmas Don came back. When I saw him my heart stopped. He was living in digs round the corner from me. I was walking behind him down Long Drive when he turned and said, 'What d'ya want? Go away.'

I was heartbroken. I fled home, howling.

'Oh Shue, I did tell you, didn't I?'

I threw myself on to the settee and stayed there all night.

Steve had been calling round nearly every evening. He appeared to be quieter than usual. He annoyed me with his silence.

'Let's go to the pictures, Sue,' Steve said one evening.

'What the hell for?'

'I want to see *Where Eagles Dare*.'

'Oh all right.'

It was pouring with rain. Steve had a huge umbrella. Even though we got drenched we had terrific fun when the umbrella blew inside out. While waiting for the bus, Steve put his arm round my shoulder. I huddled up to him.

'Sue, I've been silly.'

'Me too.'

The following day Steve took me to meet his friends Frank and Judi. They invited us to their wedding in Barnes, London. Frank and Judi had bought a flat in Harrow. Steve and I went there a number of times before they moved in. There was a lot of work to be done. We all mucked in.

One evening I opened the door to Steve. He handed me a letter neatly folded. Steve told me in the letter how he felt. When I'd finished reading it, he asked me to marry him. He said his firm, Dixons, were moving to Stevenage. We could have a house of our own if we moved with them.

Next day we went to see the vicar, who talked at length on all aspects of marriage. The wedding was booked for March 9th, 1974. We had seven weeks to make all the arrangements. There wasn't enough time to book a hall for the reception, so Mum said we could have it at home.

Because of all the previous messing around, I didn't feel I could get married in my original wedding dress. I scoured all the shopping centres I knew of, but still couldn't find anything suitable to get married in. Mum and Mrs Hill finally persuaded me to wear the one I had. I bought a new veil and tiara. Pamela was my only bridesmaid. Pauline refused to be one.

On my wedding day I awoke to see a light flurry of snow settling on the roof-tops. Pam and I went to the hairdressers. We had a manicure while waiting for our hair to dry. I was full of nerves. So was my mum. She flapped around until Pamela bodily sat her in a chair and made a cup of tea. Mum kept saying, 'I hope to God Steve has had his hair cut. I can't imagine what the vicar will say.'

I walked down the aisle on Uncle Cyril's arm. I wondered what I was doing there. I knew in my heart I didn't really want to marry Steve. We got to the altar. Uncle Cyril stepped back to the left. Looking up, I saw Steve had had his hair cut. I thought, Mum will be pleased.

It was a lovely service, even though I felt it went on a bit. Steve and I walked back up the aisle as man and wife. Steve smiled at me, saying, 'You look lovely, Sue.' He hugged me.

We stood outside the church for photos. It was bitterly cold. I could only speak through my teeth. Pam kept lifting my dress so she could get a picture of my garter.

We went back to Mum's, and everyone crowded into the living-room to drink to the bride and groom. Frank, who'd been Steve's best man, made a speech. Frank owned a disco and put on some soft music. Steve took my hand and we went round thanking people for their presents and for coming. Our faces were covered in lipstick.

Later I changed into my going-away dress. Soon it was time to leave. We'd booked two nights at the Cumberland Hotel in Harrow.

Next morning there was nothing to do, so we came home and helped Mum clear up the mess.

On Monday morning I packed my things and moved out of Mum's for the last time. Steve and I moved into Frank and Judi's. We paid them a small rent and came and went as we pleased. We lived there for about a month. Steve came home one Friday night saying, 'We've got a place in Stevenage. It's only a flat for the time being. We'll go and see it tomorrow.'

Frank and Judi came with us. We measured up for carpets and curtains. It was a small, one-bedroomed flat on the first floor. It was plenty big enough for Steve and me. I was really excited about having a home of our own. The following weekend Steve helped me choose the curtains. Our moving date was in two weeks time.

As I stood around outside Mum's house while the removal men packed our meagre belongings, I said aloud, 'This is going to be the start of a new life for me.' I kissed Mum and the old life goodbye.

18

SIOBHAN

'All these stairs to climb. I'll have to carry Sheryl. Where shall I put the buggy?' I said aloud as I looked upwards. I collapsed the buggy and hid it out of sight. 'Well, here goes.' I lifted Sheryl on to my hip.

I knocked on the office door. A lady appeared at the door and motioned me in. 'Yes?' she said.

'I would like to see Mr Bowen.'

'Have you an appointment?'

'No.'

'One moment. Take a seat.' She pointed to a small waiting area. 'This way.'

The lady led me through her office into a larger one. Behind the seat was a middle-aged man. 'What can I do for you, Mrs . . . ?' he said, looking at my left hand.

'Read. I want a divorce.'

'Yes. You will have to write a statement about the breakdown of your marriage.'

'How long will the divorce take?'

'That will depend on a number of things.'

I went home and wrote out the details of what had been happening between Steve and me. I posted it back to Mr Bowen the same day.

The following week I told Steve. 'I'm divorcing you, Steve. I've seen a solicitor.'

'Mmm.'

A letter came for Steve from Bowen and Bowen. 'There's a letter for you,' I said as I dropped it in his lap.

He sat reading the letter with a frown on his face. He tore it up and put it in the bin.

Three nights later, before he went to sleep, Steve put his arm round my waist and kissed me on the cheek. The next night he cradled me in his arms. I was so unused to affection from Steve that I found it a little strange.

This new side to Steve is great. He's taking care of himself again. In turn I put more effort into my cooking, and don't shout and scream so much.

'Mr Bowen, Steve is trying so hard lately, and I still love him. Can I call off the divorce?'

'As he is making an effort, we can delay the decree absolute for six months. Of course if things begin to slide again we can continue as we were.'

I haven't told Steve about seeing Mr Bowen again.

Steve made love to me last night. It's been over a year since we've been man and wife properly.

I'm pregnant.

I went to the diabetic clinic today. Dr Watkins says I have to go into Lister Hospital to get my diabetes controlled. I don't want to leave Steve and Sheryl, especially now, as our lives have been so good together.

My friend Helen says she'll look after Sheryl while I'm in Lister.

I'm home again after two weeks away. I've put on a lot of weight all over. I hate being so fat.

Baby doesn't kick yet and I'm 20 weeks. Sheryl kicked at 17. Don't fret, girl, no two pregnancies are alike. This baby seems much bigger than Sheryl was, probably because I don't smoke.

Twenty-two weeks. Baby moves. I love the feeling of life filling out my tummy. Steve thinks it's fascinating. He can't keep his hands off my tum. Life is lovely.

Twenty-three and a half weeks. Back to Lister. Shit. I rang Sheryl at Helen's tonight. She said, 'Mummy, are you lost? I'm lonely for you.'

'Darling, Mummy is lonely for you too.'

I let Sheryl feel baby kick. She lets me feel her baby kick too.

SIOBHAN

I went to the antenatal clinic today for the first time. They look after me all right, but they seem to have forgotten about the baby. Miss Parker says I'm only 19 weeks. I know I'm 25 weeks. I know exactly when I conceived this baby. God, please make everything all right. I'm scared.

Diabetic women tend to have large babies. Sheryl was small for a diabetic mum.

'Yes, baby will be small, like Sheryl.'

I feel like a yo-yo. In and out of Lister. Steve takes all this backwards and forwards so well. It can't be easy for him. I love him so much. I can't believe our marriage was so awful just a short while ago. Dear little Sheryl. She is so good and has taken these disturbances in her life really well. I hope all this doesn't have a bad effect on her.

Thirty-two weeks. The time has come to go into Lister until baby is born. Dr Watkins has said I can go home at weekends. I suppose that's a small consolation. Tonight I sat Sheryl on my lap and told her I was going away again. No protests. She puts all her trust in me. I wonder, what does my Sheryl think of all this?

Baby kicks constantly now.

I'm on Ward 9B, in my own little room with bathroom and toilet. The staff are terrific. Apart from my writing there's nothing to do all day. Sometimes I make the beds and change the water jugs.

I want to trade in my ticket and get off.

I took Sheryl home at the weekend. The result was devastating. She wouldn't eat. She vomited over the table. Wet the bed. In general her behaviour was atrocious. I could have shaken her. Steve, Helen and I had a chat about Sheryl. We decided that I shouldn't see her again until after the baby has been born. I think she thought that when she saw me on Friday the baby would be with me. I have to consider Sheryl first. She is the most important one in this damned rigmarole. I want out of this mess. Sheryl is getting hurt. It's all my fault.

Shut up moaning, woman. At least you know what's going on, Sheryl doesn't. I'll still ring her up. And Steve will visit her.

Thirty-three weeks. I'm obese. Fourteen stone. I know I'm pregnant, but it's not that kind of big. It's horrible being fat. Moan. Moan. Moan.

Thirty-six weeks. Miss Parker came today. She and three doctors felt my stomach. They all say baby is small, even though I'm huge. Ooh, I'm getting strange vibes. Sister said I've got to go for an ultrasound scan on Monday.

Steve bought Sheryl a large blue, red and white Smurf. He took her for a ride into Weston. She sat on the back seat hugging the Smurf.

I had the scan this morning. They say baby is definitely small. I hate them. They're only saying these things to worry me.

They should be inducing me next week. I don't have Caesareans. They're stalling so they have to section me. I will not have it. I'm frightened of operations.

Thirty-seven weeks and one day. I've been transferred to the North Herts. Maternity Unit. I won't be able to see my Steve in the evenings. North Herts. is strict with its rules. Visiting finishes at 8.30 p.m. Steve doesn't get out of work until 9 p.m. It's hard luck that we'll miss each other.

Stop feeling sorry for yourself, Sue, you'll be home for the weekend, then all this should be over some time next week.

I had an X-ray today and another scan. 'You've got your dates wrong, Susan, by at least four weeks,' Miss Parker said.

'Look here, I know when I conceived this baby. There's no other time it could have happened.'

Two days later, Miss Parker said, 'We'll have to section you, Susan.'

'No.' I was on my feet, yelling.

I will not have a Caesarean. I let them give me the amniocentesis test twice. They put a large needle into my tummy and drew off the fluid. As I said before, diabetic women have large babies, but with immature lungs. The amniocentesis test enables them to check if the baby's lungs are mature enough to induce labour. Miss Parker has already told me that baby's lungs are all right. I'm going to give birth normally. I will not let that woman make me have an operation.

Oh I'm so scared. I want to go home to my little family.

Miss Parker told Maggie (the social worker) she thinks the placenta is dying. That's why baby is so small. If I have baby normally and the placenta packs up altogether, baby will almost certainly die.

God, I want a chat with you. I've never had to make a hard decision before. Inside my tummy I have a baby that Steve and I made when we were happy together. I'm sure it's a girl. I've never held her or looked at her, but she's been in my tummy for exactly 38 weeks now and there's a bond between us. I need your help and wisdom. God, you know why my baby is small and why I'm frightened of operations. Tell me I should have a Caesarean and I will. Please God, make my baby all right, and give her mummy and daddy the strength to cope, whatever happens.

I rang Helen earlier and told her what was going on. She rang Steve at work and he came straight here. We saw the X-ray. Baby looked small, but otherwise just a baby to us. I went home with Steve. We got into bed fully clothed and held each other tightly. We called in to see Helen. Sheryl was in bed.

I feel calmer now. I'm so tired.

I had a Caesarean and sterilization operation on Friday November 10th, 1978. Steve came early that morning. He walked with me to the theatre doors, holding my hand.

I opened my eyes to see Steve, his eyes wet with tears.

'My tummy hurts.'

Steve sat on the bed.

'Was it a girl, darling? Is she all right?'

Silence.

'What's wrong?'

'She's got spina bifida, Sue.'

'Oh no.'

Silence.

'Spina bifida. Spina bifida. Spina fucking bifida. Oh no, my poor baby.'

Frank Hinde, the paediatrician, came in. 'Sue, it's Frank, the baby has spina bifida. We don't know how bad it is yet. We'll have to wait for Great Ormond Street's verdict.'

'Steve, cuddle me.'

Sister told Steve to lie down beside me. She left us alone and we cried together.

'I love you, Sue.'

'And I love you, darling.'

Next morning they took me to Special Care in a wheelchair. She is beautiful, just like Sheryl.

'Hello, baby.' I sat with tears streaming down my face, huffing up the glass on the incubator. 'Oh God, please protect her because I can't,' I prayed aloud. I mustn't get involved with her. I mustn't start something I can't continue. Steve, where are you? I need you. I don't know how I should feel. I'm in a little ward with three other mums and their babies.

God, do you remember when I got pregnant? All the things I said about not wanting to be. Did this happen because I said all those things? I know it won't change anything now, but I didn't mean it. I was frightened and I'm still frightened. I can't help thinking it's all my fault. Look what I've done now. I should have been left to rot in St Bernard's. God, I hate me — as everyone else will when they know what's happened.

We have called baby Siobhan Helen. I asked Sister if we could have her baptized today. Steve, Sister, a nurse, me and the vicar were there. Steve held Siobhan for the first time. His face was a picture.

Siobhan won't feed. What shall I do? She probably knows I don't like her. I do really. I'm just scared of getting involved with her. What if I can't manage? I don't know anything about spina bifida.

She won't take the 1 p.m. feed either. I don't care. If she wants to play silly buggers that's up to her. I'm going to have my afternoon nap.

Now she won't take the 5 p.m. feed.

I've waited until 9 p.m. to ensure that she's really hungry. But no, she struggles and pushes me away.

'Now listen, Siobhan, stop this nonsense. If anyone's going

to do any pushing and shoving it will be me. I'm your mum.
You're my little girl . . .' I hugged her tightly to my chest —
'. . . and I love you.' I felt a warmth spreading through me,
and tears were trickling down my cheeks.

I gently laid Siobhan in her cot and rushed down the
corridor to the phone. I dialled my number. Steve answered.
Without preamble I said, 'Siobhan won't feed today. She
pushes me away. Yes, she does. Come and get me. You don't
want me either. Don't you love me? I love you. Please come
and get me. I need you to hold me tight. I'm so frightened. She
doesn't love me and I love her so much. I didn't want to. I
almost made myself hate her, but I can't help it now. She's got
to me and I do love her and she doesn't want me, she pushes
me away. I miss you, darling, and Sheryl. I know you do. I'm
sorry. I can't help it. I love you too. Ni-night.'

I went back to Special Care. I lifted Siobhan and cuddled
her to me. Thank you, God, for making me strong.

Frank told me today that Siobhan has hydrocephalus (water
on the brain), which is connected to spina bifida. I still can't
believe they're talking about my baby. To me she's normal.
She looks normal. She feels normal. And apart from yesterday
she feeds normally. Perhaps it isn't really happening. Bash.
Bash. Kick. Wake up, dopey. Nightmare's over.

Helen brought Sheryl to visit today. How good it felt to hug
her and chatter away. To be a child with her for half an hour.

Steve came in tonight. I hadn't seen him since Sunday. He's
grown a moustache. Looks . . . Mmm. It was good to have his
arms round me. I miss him dreadfully. He was downhearted
when I told him what Frank had said about the water on the
brain. All this will either make us or break us. I never thought
this would happen.

It won't happen to me.

It's a strange feeling. My head feels a long way away — like
I'm standing watching it happen to someone else. I can talk
about it. I can write about it. I can even cope with it now. The
spina bifida I mean, not Siobhan. They're not the same, even
though they go together.

I'm going home in two days. I've been away for eight weeks

today. Siobhan won't be with me, but I'm prepared emotionally.

I'm going home tomorrow.

I gave Siobhan the breast before she left. I washed and dressed her. Holding her tight, I sang, 'If you ever go across the sea to Ireland.' I was holding her on my shoulder. She craned her neck to look into my face, then fell forward on to my cheek. She sucked my cheek. She kissed me. I can still feel that wet kiss.

The ambulance men put Siobhan into an egg-shaped incubator. She was asleep and didn't see me crying. As they wheeled her away, I felt they were taking — NO, *wrenching* — a part of me away from my body. I'm not ashamed to cry. I'm frightened for my baby. I'm worried for her future, and God, what if I can't cope with the future.

God, don't let them hurt her any more. I can only do so much. Please don't hurt her any more.

I love Siobhan so much. She has opened avenues in my heart that I didn't know existed.

I got dressed and rang for a taxi to take me to Helen's. I said goodbye to everyone, wishing with all my heart that I was arriving to give birth and things were different. I'm always wishing for something. Siobhan won't suffer while I'm her mum.

Now I'm home I'm in a daze. My breasts are full and a constant reminder.

Siobhan had her meningocele removed today. I said I'd be prepared emotionally, but I'm not. My head feels far, far away. Sheryl gives me lots of cuddles. Darling, you're my silver lining.

We went to Great Ormond Street to see Siobhan. Her head was bandaged like a sheikh's. I wanted to hold her to my bosom, but I wasn't allowed to. I could only hold her flat on my lap. The nurse told us why, but I can't remember. Sheryl was mesmerized. She let Siobhan clutch her finger. It's the first time she's been so close to her.

I asked Dr Oakes about Siobhan's prognosis. He said that

when they removed the meningocele there was brain matter in it which they pushed back into her head, hoping it was viable. I told him that Steve and I felt she might be a bit backward, but otherwise all right. He said he could show us a child with a brain the size of a little fingernail, who could do everything that Siobhan could. At six months the baby would progress no further. The mental age would stay the same.

Oh God, I'm scared. I feel like I haven't stopped being scared for a long time.

I'm desperately lonely for Siobhan. First I want to be home, and now I'm home I want to be with Siobhan.

What an awful dull ache I have in my chest.

December 6th, and Siobhan is home for the first time. In her own cot. In her own home. I feel complete again. She still feeds well, even though I bottle-feed her because my own milk supply has run out.

I was always in a hurry when Sheryl was a baby. It's different with Siobhan; I've got more time to cuddle her and be her mum. I showed her the snow today. I put a bit on her hand. She shuddered. We'll show those silly experts. Six months will never come. We'll pull through.

December 18th. Siobhan had to go back to Great Ormond Street to see if she needs a shunt fitted to drain the water on the brain. When we got there we were told by Dr Oakes, 'You've got the wrong day. Come back tomorrow.'

'I've got a letter here telling me to come today. I don't live round the corner, and even if I did this is your mistake. Now I insist you look at Siobhan.' I had fed Siobhan at 7 a.m. By now it was midday. She was hungry and in a dreadful state. Even her dummy wouldn't pacify her. I asked if she could have a bottle.

'Oh no, she can't eat before a brain scan,' the nurse informed me.

Her screams were wretched. I felt so inadequate.

At 3 p.m. we were told by a doctor the scanner had broken down. He told us, 'Of course, we could measure her head, which is another way of detecting hydrocephalus, except there's nothing to compare the measurements with as we've mislaid Siobhan's notes.'

Siobhan was beside herself with hunger. I said, 'Right, the scanner's gone kaput. You've lost her notes and I'm feeding her now, like it or not.'

At this a nurse came running, saying the scanner was working again. Steve and I were given protective garments to wear. A technician put Siobhan's head into a leather cap with a strap tied under her chin. She put some honey on her dummy to keep her quiet.

After the scan, we went back to the ward and Siobhan drank two three-ounce bottles of milk. Dr Oakes came at 4.15 p.m. and said that they would need to fit a shunt. We could leave her there and go home. I don't want her to have another operation. But I want her to be all right. I know she needs the shunt and I can't stay with her. Again I feel that heaviness in my chest as I lift her into my arms.

'I shall think of you every minute of every day. I love you, baby,' I whispered into her ear.

I couldn't see for tears as we made our way home. If only life didn't have to hurt so much.

Steve should have gone to work that morning at 6 a.m. It was Saturday January 13th, 1979 — just over 18 months ago. For some reason Steve turned off the alarm, snuggled up to me and went back to sleep.

At 9.10 a.m. I woke. I commented to Steve that Siobhan was a good girl, sleeping right through the night. I stepped into my dressing-gown. I went down to get Siobhan. It was eerie and cold in the living-room. I shook myself, saying aloud, 'Get your baby up, Susan.'

I'd always lain her on her tummy. I went to the carry-cot and picked her up. 'Ooh, Mummy's bubber is chilly,' I said as I rubbed her back. I went into the kitchen and switched on the kettle.

Years flashed by. I spoke lots of words, rubbing frantically at her cold body, willing her to warm up. When I looked down at her face, I saw it was squashed and ghostly white down the middle. All the blood had drained to the sides.

My beautiful baby had died.

My mind flashed back. I was stepping into my dressing-gown.

'Mummy will get the doctor.' I laid her back in her carry-cot.

I rang 999. Steve came down the stairs, looked at her and shouted, 'She's dead. She's smothered.'

I couldn't stand any more, and sank to the floor. 'You fucking bastard, God. You've taken her away,' I whimpered into the carpet.

I was stepping into my dressing-gown. Change it. Make the story different. I want Siobhan back.

'You bastard. You've made my heart hurt so much for so long. I hate you. I hate you. You've played a nasty trick on me.'

I can't seem to get my mind into order. Do you care? No. Why should you care? I want to go away. I don't want to think any more.

Eighteen months have gone by and I still ache for her. How can I dismiss her when I loved her so much? Nine weeks isn't a long time. But that nine weeks was Siobhan's lifetime, and to me it was forever.

Everything about her was beautiful. Even her spina bifida. Does that make sense?

I told the undertakers to embalm her. I had to see her beautiful again before she was buried. The morning of the funeral they brought her home. I held Steve's hand and we found hers. She was like wax. We put her baby teddy in her right hand. We kissed her cheeks. They were like cold peaches. They had made her beautiful again.

I had to use every force in my body not to pick her up out of the coffin and hold her to my bosom. God, how could you take her away from me? Why did you give her to me? You knew you wouldn't let me keep her.

'Why my baby? Why?'

The snow was really thick the day of the funeral. It was cold, and my heart felt colder.

When they lowered her into the ground they took a huge chunk of me. This brought forth a torrent of tears. I sobbed loud and unashamedly. Steve's tears trickled down my neck as he wrapped his arms around me and nestled close.

Mum was pulling me away from Steve, saying, 'Come on, Shue. It's all over. Come home now.'

'I want to stay with Steve. Let me stay with you, Steve. I want Steve.'

Steve held on to me tighter.

'It's all over, Shue.'

Over. It will never be over. Never ever.

Days later I bought a little bush. With my bare hands I scrabbled away the snow and planted it. That is our Siobhan bush.

People don't talk about Siobhan. I express my feelings here, or with Steve, darling Steve. Every day I mentally go through the process of digging her out of the ground. Holding her tight to warm my heart again.

She's cold out there in the snow. My poor little love. Darling, I'm so sorry I didn't have more time with you. I wish things had been different.

Hurry and come home, Steve. I need your love.

EPILOGUE

I'm sitting at my dining-room table with my typewriter in front of me, wondering how to conclude my memories.

I have been out in society for 15 years now. The years I lived in St Bernard's were an education for me. I learnt that my mind and body could accept all types of people, all types of behaviour and most situations. It gave me a resilience and an understanding that people are different. Even the 'normal' people can behave strangely. As an ex-inmate of St Bernard's I can truly say, 'There are more nutters out than in.'

My marriage to Steve is bliss now, after a difficult start. He has sustained me and supported me through the trauma of recalling my experiences.

When I was 21 and newly married, I began to write down my life in St Bernard's. I did this as a cleansing project. I had to get it out of my system, but I didn't know anyone here in Stevenage who would listen. Besides, this was my new life, not to be clogged up with the past.

When I was 27, Steve and I were over the worst and as happy as we could be under the circumstances of losing Siobhan. I dumped all the writings in a drawer and forgot about them, until I went to see Dr Morrish one day and he said, 'Sue, why don't you write about how you feel?' I told him I had once. He asked to see it.

I dug it all out and sent it to Dr Morrish. When I next saw him he asked if he could show it to someone he knew. Later he introduced me to John Fairfax, a tutor of authors, who has been invaluable in helping me edit and put my writings into perspective without them losing their meaning.

Yes, it's been painful to dredge it all up again, but I've been left with a feeling of worthiness. Yes, it was worth getting it out of my system. I feel cleaner than I've ever felt.

Siobhan came at a time when things were still shaky between Steve and me. She cemented our marriage and gave us both some common ground. We both loved her and lost her. We still grieve for her, nearly seven years on. There will always be a gap in my heart and life that belongs to Siobhan. Again I learnt something from loving her. Nearly everything I've done since has been an extension of her, the best being the six years we've been fostering children.

Sheryl has emerged unscathed into a lovely young girl who Steve and I are extremely proud of.

My relationship with Mum is much better. I still don't love my mum, but I like and respect her. Her life has not been easy. She is still suffering in many ways.

I used to look back and resent losing my youth. Now when I look back I don't regret what happened. It has enriched me. I'm a better person for my experiences.

THE MEDICAL RECORD

Explanatory text by Dr Leslie Morrish

NOTE

The letters and reports that follow are reproduced by kind permission of
the doctors concerned. Their publication here does not imply that
Dr Blair or any of the other doctors necessarily confirms or upholds the
contents of this book.

THE MEDICAL RECORD

In February 1965 Susan was sent to hospital by her General Practitioner. The registrar reports back.

Hillingdon Hospital
5th March.

Dear Dr MacGreevy,

Re: Susan Read

Admitted: 5.2.65.   Discharged: 20.2.65

Diagnosis: Diabetes Mellitus.

This child was seen in the outpatients with a six weeks history of frequency of micturition. There was no dysuria, but it was noted that she also had polydypsia taking 5-6 pints of fluid a day. She had recently lost weight. A cousin is a diabetic.

On examination she was a rather thin girl apyrexial, not dehydrated with no anaemia. Chest and cardio-vascular system were normal, the abdomen was soft, there were no palpable masses and the central nervous system appeared intact. Her urine showed 2% sugar on clinitest and acetone was present. The blood sugar was 530 ml/100, 3½ hours after a meal.

Her haemoglobin was 88% white blood count 3,400 per cmm, 58% neutrophils. A Heaf test was negative. Urine on microscopy showed only a few leococytes. Chest x-ray was clear.

She was treated with soluble insulin initially requiring approximately 28 units daily on which she became ketone free. However, 2% sugar persisted and it was necessary eventually to give her 32 units of lente insulin daily. She was taught to give her own injections and manages very well. She was discharged on the 19.2.65 and will be seen again as an out-patient. Free diet has been allowed.

D.B. Soutter
Paediatric Registrar.

However, control of the diabetic imbalance was not satisfactory. Further help was sought from the Post-Graduate Teaching Hospital at Hammersmith.

Hammersmith Hospital
19th May, 1965.

Dear Dr B.K.P. MacGreevy.
Re: Susan Read.

Thank you for referring this young girl whom I saw at the diabetic clinic on the 14th May. Her diabetes had presented with thirst, polyuria, and weight loss four months ago. There was a family history of diabetes occurring in a cousin on the father's side.

Since December she has been treated at the Hillingdon Hospital on a free diet and lente insulin 36 units daily. In recent weeks her control, as assessed by home-testing, has been less satisfactory with frequent 2% glycosuria and what sounds to have been frequent hypoglycaemia episodes occurring in the early hours of the morning.

On examination she was a thin girl, wt. 5st. 1lb. Apart from a functional systolic murmur at the left systolic edge, physical examination was normal.

Stable control in this age group is very difficult, but particularly so when there is no disciplined dietary regulation. Both she and her mother have been instructed in the necessity for adhering to a 180 g carbohydrate intake and I have not altered the dose of insulin until I can assess her response to this regime in one week's time.

K.E.W. Melvin, M.R.C.P., M.R.A.C.P.
Registrar to Prof. Russell Fraser.

Susan was undisciplined in her behaviour and in her diet. Her diabetes remained uncontrolled. Her mother pleaded for help, so Susan was seen by the psychiatrist Dr Hersov. The unruly behaviour continued. Susan, it was believed, would do better if she were away from home. So would her family. Dr Hersov was unable to arrange a suitable placement at a children's home or adolescent unit. He wrote to Dr Blair, consultant at St Bernard's Hospital.

Hammersmith Hospital
2nd February, 1966.

Dear Dr. Blair,

Re: *Susan Read*

... She was referred to me from the Diabetic Clinic of this hospital with the problem of severely disturbed behaviour since the summer of last year. This led to her exclusion from her secondary modern school in October and she has just been excluded from a special class for maladjusted children in Hillingdon. She is at present at home with nothing to do.

The sequence of events is as follows: that she was diagnosed in January, 1965, as suffering from diabetes mellitus and has been under the care of the Diabetic Clinic here for some time.

Her present dosage of insulin is as follows: 40 units soluble a.m. and 24 units soluble + 12 units NPH p.m. She is also on a 180 G CHO diet (45-10-40-20-45-20).

She was fully investigated in hospital recently to see whether her behaviour disorder was the result of uncontrolled diabetes, but this was not found to be the case. She has obviously had a psychological response to having diabetes and having to treat herself, but she does give herself injections and take responsibility for her diet, although this clearly does vary with her mood. Sometimes she will miss out an injection or overeat. However, in general she is under good control.

The family situation is as follows:— her father died suddenly on 13th March 1965, from a coronary thrombosis. He had a previous attack one year prior to his death and was off work for eight months. His death came as a great shock to the whole family (there are three other children) but seems to have affected Susan more than the others as she depended on his warmth and interest a great deal more and now misses the support and control which he provided. Mrs Read was herself depressed following her husband's death and is at the moment quite unable to cope with Susan and her behaviour. Susan seems to hold the whole family physically to ransom, is demanding, disobedient, abusive, uses bad language so much so that Mrs Read has reached the end of her tether and feels she cannot cope any longer. Indeed, we have been worried about her own state, and Mrs Maser P.S.W. with me has seen her regularly for support.

I have been seeing Susan weekly since November and at interview the most striking thing is her pressure of talk, which appears inconsequential but usually reflects her current pre-occupations. At the beginning she talked mostly about her father but she has a continued concern with marriage and sexuality in general. There was a time when she took to asking older men to take her for a drive and she is still provocative to older men in terms of her conversation and the jokes she makes. She seems always able to extricate herself from a situation which she has provoked, but I fear that her luck might not hold all the time. I do feel that the reason behind this behaviour is connected with the loss of her father, and her need to have a relationship with an older man as a father substitute. This has sometimes come into the therapeutic situation but she has stopped trying to be provocative with me since this was pointed out to her.

At interview she has been able to reveal the depression behind her restless, talkative exhibitionist behaviour. However, in recent weeks her conversation has been more inconsequential than usual, she has taken to using new strange words that she makes up and also shows a repetitive grimace of protruding her lower jaw, wrinkling her nose and opening her mouth. She has shown shiffing tics in the past, but this is more severe than ever before.

A psychological test on 15th December, 1965, gave the following result:

W.I.S.C.   Full Scale   I.Q. 88
"   Verbal Scale   I.Q. 97
"   Performance Scale I.Q. 79
Reading Age: 13 2/12 years
Spelling Age: 12 3/12 years

My original diagnosis was of an affective disorder, with the depressive element more prominent although concealed by restless talkativeness. I feel this still is probably the case but I am beginning to wonder whether there is a more severe psychotic element entering into her behaviour recently.

I feel very strongly that it would be better for her to be treated away from home, in her own interests and the interests of her family. She needs comprehensive care because of her diabetes, although this does not provide a real problem of medical management. Many avenues of placement have been explored through hospitals and local authority services, but these have proved unsuccessful. It seems imperative that she be admitted somewhere where she can be treated, as I feel the longer the situation is allowed to continue the more difficult it will be to help her.

I telephoned Dr Dobson's (the Medical Officer of Health for Hillingdon) department today to ask whether a welfare officer could visit the home this evening or to-morrow morning to make arrangements for an escort or in terms of transport for Susan and her mother to come and see you on Friday. I spoke to one of Dr Dobson's deputies and he agreed to make this arrangement.

I must again thank you for your help with this child and I look forward to hearing from you.

L.A. Hersov MD DPM
Honorary Consultant in Psychological Medicine

Susan was admitted to Ellis Ward.

Hospital Note 4.2.1966.
Has been very disturbed since her fathers on March 30th. (sic)
Displays various twitches.
Says she has been expelled from school for saying 'shut your gob'.
Teacher was horrible to me.
Went to another school where they said she was mental.
Talks easily.
Finds it difficult to get to sleep. 'I was in a coma the other morning'
Diabetic since last year.
Father had his first coronary 1964.
Has difficulty in getting to sleep.
Brother is 4 years old.
Has been seeing Dr Hirsoff at Hammersmith Hospital since October 1965.

Hypomanic Character disorder.
Haloperidal 1.5 mgm tds
Sod. Amytal gms 3 nocte
Sol. Insulin 10 units mane
N.P.H. 2 units.

14th Feb. 1966.

In a cross mood this morning complaining about 'Grannie' (another pt. who disciplined her as much as possible) 'Why does she do all that jazz? — charming — I'm trying to stop bad language . . .' Asked to be allowed to dust the paper perforator on the table 'I like everything to be nice and clean'. 'Why don't I get depressed? . . . I do in my mind'. 'I try to be kind to Grannie . . .'.

Patient says she's here 'to get better of my mentalness'.
'I've got a cranky brain . . .'.
Before admission 'Little fits' (shows shaking of hands).
'At school they said "Here comes that mental nit" '.

17th Feb. 1966

Patient had an epileptiform fit this morning.

The epileptic fits led to a request for neurological opinion.

ST. BERNARDS HOSPITAL   10th March, 1966

Dear Dr Melvin.

Thank you very much for seeing this girl in connection with the two epileptic fits which she has had here, and for a general review.

Her mother informs me that there have been several episodes in which the girl has lost consciousness, or has had some kind of fit. The first occasion, about the first week in August 1965, while staying in Haywards Heath, the child could not be roused in the morning. A doctor was called and gave an injection. The second episode about the last week in August 1965 her mother was wakened by noise which the child was making, she noticed that her arms and legs were moving and she was frothing at the mouth. Her mother was able to give her some glucose to drink after some time and after this she appeared to be her normal self after about 15 mintues.

A specimen of urine tested at the time showed no glucose. A third occasion occurred three nights later and the events were similar. The patient's mother again gave her a glucose drink. The fourth occasion was about two months later and her mother reports that it was a mild episode occurring in the early hours of the morning. The fifth episode occurred about 7 a.m. on the day before Susan's admission here. Her mother found the child on the floor of the bedroom, her sister said that she had been making funny noises. She may have been unconscious for a time. It was about half an hour after her mother found her before she was much improved and for about another hour she complained of seeing double and of things appearing far away.

Susan's mother thinks that there may have been other episodes which were unwitnessed, for there were occasions when she found Susan not to be quite normal first thing in the morning, she appeared vague and a bit confused and was unable to answer questions properly.

On the 17th February, the Night Nurse reported that Susan had a major fit at 5 a.m. Blood sugar was found to be 50 mgm per 100 ml at 10 a.m. On the 21st February, Susan had a major fit at 12.15 a.m.

Susan appears to be gradually settling here. There have been episodes when her behaviour has been extremely troublesome and provoking towards other patients. There was some improvement after we commenced Haloperidol, 1.5 mg t.i.d.

Yours sincerely,

C.L. Lovett
Assistant Psychiatrist

Hospital Note:
29th March.   Reported yesterday to have been v. troublesome — aggressive.
Struck a nurse on face with slipper.
Urine heavily loaded with sugar — pt. reported to eat sweets and biscuits in addition to her diet.

Interviewed
Tense, emotional, tearful.
'Stuck here for two months, everybody else goes home for week-ends — — — '
Says she doesn't know what happened yesterday.

13th April.   Susan has continued to be very difficult in the ward. She is emotionally very unstable and usually fatuously euphoric. She impulsively attacks patients and hurts them and today hit a pt. in bed and another patient who is up but who is pregnant.
No longer fit for Ellis Ward. Transfer to 19F.
NB   Her mother was phoned and consents to this move.

Ward 19 was a locked ward for refractory cases. Patients who were a danger to themselves or to others would sometimes need the security that locks could offer. It certainly eased the onus on nursing staff — and with nurses too thinly spread, such relief was welcome.

Many patients, it is sad to relate, considered incarceration in a locked ward as punishment — and this despite being assured by the doctors that it was not so. But then patients were there because they tended to see things out of proportion, so it is not surprising that the wisdom of restraint often escaped them.

Unfortunately, some of the staff also regarded such restriction as punishment and were known to use the threat of transfer as a means of ensuring good behaviour.

14th April.   Quite well behaved.
Says she does have a reason for attacking people.

15th April.   Transfer back to Ellis but if she misbehaves again she will go back to 19F.

Dr Blair was seriously concerned by this turn of events. To have a young girl on his admission ward because nowhere else had the facility to care for her was itself bad enough; to have to lock her up in the company of seriously and chronically disturbed psychotics was a step to be contemplated with trepidation.

There was in addition the continued risk of sexual encounter — and the newspapers were unlikely to understand the dilemma.

The doctors at the Hammersmith shared this unease.

16th June, 1966

Dear Dr Blair,

Please find enclosed a copy of my letter to Dr Pallis seeking further advice about Susan Read's EEG abnormalities. When I saw her last on the 10th of June I was encouraged by what appeared to be a definite improvement in her manner. I was worried however at her mother's account of Susan's exposure to the same sexual dangers that prompted us to seek institutional care in the first instance. There may, of course, be little truth in what was said but I feel that you should know that Susan informs her mother that she is frequently a close spectator of intercourse between patients, and that on two or three occasions she herself has been threatened. I am well aware of Susan's unusual interest in these matters and accept of course, that she is likely to flights of fancy in this field. This cannot, however, go without mention.

Yours sincerely,

K.E.W. Melvin M.R.A.C.P.
Registrar to Professor Russell Fraser.

Dr Blair tried again to find a more suitable placement. He wrote to the local Medical Officer of Health and to Dr Hersov at the Hammersmith, who in turn wrote to the Regional Hospital Board.

22nd June, 1966

Dear Dr Dobson,

Thank you for your letter about this patient. I must admit I am extremely worried about her. She presents the most difficult therapeutic and social problem. She suffers from diabetes, has

159

some cerebral dysrhythmia and her behaviour renders her difficult to manage. It is not easy to make a psychiatric diagnosis and I am reluctant to assess her as a psychopath, although in the light of the failure of her symptoms to improve, this would seem the most probable nature of her ailment.

I enclose a copy of my letter to Dr Hersov, which is self-explanatory. I would be very grateful indeed if you could send a social worker to see Mrs Read as an urgency. She is, I think, on the verge of a nervous breakdown herself and she feels lonely, isolated and without any help from anybody other than the doctors here and at Hammersmith Hospital. She has neither friends nor relatives to whom she can turn for assistance.

I would also appreciate it if you could contact the Education Authorities in your area and ask them what they could suggest for Miss Read. I would be pleased to discuss the matter with them if they could visit us at the hospital.

Yours sincerely

Donald Blair, M.A. MD D.P.M.
Consultant Psychiatrist

22nd June, 1966

Dear Dr Hersov,

Thank you for your letter regarding this girl. She has certainly presented us with very difficult problems. On the one hand she can be charming and likeable and even lovable and in such a state is popular with the patients. On the other hand outspoken, self-opinionated and irresponsible. I think she has made a little progress since she has been here but I am apprehensive about what would happen if she returned home. I really have only been willing to keep her here for the following reasons:

1. To relieve her mother of the tremendous strain of looking after her.
2. In the hope that her behaviour would improve sufficiently for me to write a good report to the Education Authorities so that they could place her appropriately at a school next term.

3. Because no other alternative accommodation has been available for her, as you have explained to me.

The situation now is utterly desperate. She does not want to stay here any longer, but mother does not want to have her home in her present state and I think it will be almost impossible to find a school that would accept her. If she did return home I think she would be unmanageable for her mother who is very worried about the prospects of having to look after her. I am retaining her for a little longer but I am afraid that there will be no option but to discharge her home in the fairly near future, if no other alternative can be found. In this case she would almost certainly have to be taken before the Court in the near future as unmanageable and then it would be up to them to find a suitable school for her — presumably it would be in an approved school.

I am going to write to the Medical Officer of Health of Hillingdon Borough to ask him to be sure to send a social worker to help poor Mrs Read in all the predicaments that face her, and this refers not only to Susan but to the elder sister as well.

Incidentally, she has had two E.E.G. tracings made at your hospital and I am still waiting for the final verdict about them but I gather they are diffusely and grossly abnormal although not typically epileptic.

Yours sincerely,

Donald Blair, M.A. MD D.P.M.
Consultant Psychiatrist

5th July, Noisy and unruly in F. Ellis.
Ran out and had to be brought back by two nurses.
Her sister Pamela's boyfriend is in Conway Ward.
Pt's mother seen.
Patient to be transferred to F19.

15th July, 1966

Dear Coleman,

I enclose herewith a copy of a letter I have written to Dr Hersov about this case, which I think is self-explanatory. The whole situation is really tragic. We have done our level best for her here and originally I thought there was a chance that her mental condition would improve but there remains a behaviour problem and the difficulties confronting us will be obvious to you in reading my report and that of Dr Hersov. Incidentally, there is one point I would like to make, namely that she is very good at administering her own Insulin, and would be very co-operative in any school or institution where she resided. It would only be necessary for a member of the staff to see that she had her Insulin at the right time. There might be a slight danger that in a moment of negativism or defiance she would not take the injection or the right dose if left to her own devices. It is really imperative that we get something done about this girl and unfair to her and to everyone else to keep her at this hospital much longer.

Yours sincerely

Donald Blair M.A. MD D.P.M.

P.S.   I have just received your letter to me about this patient but I am still sending this one, which I think is self-explanatory. With reference to the type of unit suitable to her this is a matter on which I want your decision because to be honest I am not myself clear regarding the units available for this very unusual type of case. I think that after reading my report about her you may be able to reach an appropriate decision.

10th August, 1966

Dear Dr Dobson,

I enclose a copy of my letter to Dr Kenton and his reply.

In these circumstances there is no alternative but to ask you to implement his recommendations so that Susan will be able to start school in September. I am afraid that in all the circumstances prevailing the responsibility must be yours and if complaints continue to be made I can only draw attention to my efforts on Susan's behalf and the recommendations of the Regional Psychiatrist. Needless to say, I realise the difficulties with which you are faced but it does seem to me that unless you can now arrange for her admission to a school of the type Dr Kenton mentions the matter may actually get as far as a parliamentary question by the local M.P. I know Mrs Read is extremely dissatisfied with the whole situation and so are her friends and I think they will not have any alternative but to resort to their M.P. if nothing can be done along the lines that Dr Kenton has suggested.

I am sorry to have to confront you with such a difficult problem but would be grateful to have a reply from you at your earliest convenience. I am not sure whether any of your social workers have been to visit Susan, but I would of course be willing to discuss the whole case with you or any members of your staff.

Yours sincerely,

Donald Blair M.A. MD D.P.M.
Consultant Psychiatrist

LONDON BOROUGH OF HILLINGDON

19th September 1966

Dear Dr MacGreevy
　　　　re *Susan READ dob 31.10.53*

Since the 4th February of this year Susan has been placed informally at St Bernard's Hospital, Southall. At that time Dr Blair, Consultant Psychiatrist at the hospital, agreed to take Susan after the facts of the case had been presented to him by Dr Hersov of the Hammersmith Hospital. As you know, at that time, placing away from home became imperative and it highlighted the lamentable lack of facilities for seriously mentally disturbed children, especially those in their early teens. Since that time the Local Education Authority has tried to place Susan in every available boarding establishment for maladjusted pupils but always without success. Pressure has also been brought to bear upon the Regional Psychiatrist of the North-West Regional Hospital Board so that he might find a place for Susan within the hospital set-up of the National Health Service; again without success.

In August the Local Authority addressed a letter to the Minister of Health setting out the immense problem of Susan's case and asking him to provide an answer. So far there has been no reply.

On Tuesday next, 27th September, at 11.00 a.m. a meeting has been arranged at St Bernard's Hospital between the Senior Medical and Educational Officers of this Authority and Dr Blair, Consultant Psychiatrist at St Bernard's. The object is to discuss Susan's future. If convenient to you, your presence would be very welcomed.

I thought that I ought to let you have this information in case Susan is discharged to her home at any time, and once more the child's treatment becomes your responsibility.

O.E. DOBSON
MEDICAL OFFICER OF HEALTH

LONDON BOROUGH OF HILLINGDON
EDUCATION COMMITTEE

13th October 1966

Dear Dr Dobson

Following on from the conference we had at St Bernard's Hospital about Susan, I got in touch with the Adolescent Unit near Southampton and have had a reply from them that unfortunately they are not able to offer Susan a vacancy and cannot take cases out of Wessex.

I have also been in touch with another Unit — The Ingrebourne Center, St George's Hospital, Hornchurch, where they do occasionally take adolescents, but again they are not able to offer Susan a vacancy.

So it does seem that there will be no alternative but for Susan to return home and attend Manor School on a trial basis.

I do think, however, that it is important for the Children's Department to be fully informed about this case. I am also writing to Dr Blair to say I was not able to obtain a vacancy for Susan in an In-patients Unit.

MARGARET MORGAN
MEDICAL DIRECTOR

MEDICAL OFFICER OF HEALTH

21st October 1966

Dear Dr Hersov

A conference with regard to this child's future was held at St Bernard's Hospital on Tuesday, 27th September at 11.00 a.m.

It was agreed then that Dr Morgan, Psychiatrist, would contact some Adolescent Units of which she was aware to see if they could offer a vacancy for Susan. Dr Morgan has done this without success.

It is now almost certain that Dr Blair, Consultant Psychiatrist, will be returning Susan to her home environment in the very near future.

I have alerted the Borough Children's Officer that Susan might well be brought to his attention as being beyond control.

In the meantime I would be very grateful if you would please let me know if you would be prepared to see Susan occasionally and particularly if a crisis occurred.

Your observations would be very much appreciated.

O.C. Dobson
MEDICAL OFFICER OF HEALTH

TO THE SENIOR MEDICAL OFFICER
NORTH WEST REGION MEDICAL BOARD

17th December 1966

Dear Sir,

Thank you for your letter of the 7th December. The basic situation about this girl I have already described in the letters you mention and I have no reason to change the views I expressed there. I am, however, pleased to tell you that her behaviour has improved greatly since she has been for the last few months in a closed ward — this naturally does not mean that she stays in the ward all the time, she is allowed lots of freedom and goes to Art Therapy etc. The discipline she received there was firmer than that she received in the previous open ward, where it was difficult to control her, and she has responded well. In the ward she appears to be happy, co-operative, fond of the Sisters and Staff and on the whole quite well adjusted. She is understandably becoming somewhat restive and repeatedly asks me what arrangements are being made for her future. I understand from her mother that at home she is very easily manageable and less of a problem than she was. She has since she has been here matured both physically and mentally. She administers her own Insulin carefully and effectively.

While mentally her recent progress in this hospital has been satisfactory, one cannot be sure how she will conduct herself when she is in the world at large again. Nevertheless, the stage has in my opinion been reached where one can now consider schools for her that would not have been previously suitable. I think it might even be possible to give her a chance at an ordinary school near her home provided that the staff were reasonably tactful, understanding and helpful. If it were done it would have to be with her understanding and everybody elses that should she not co-operate and comply to regulations properly, boarding school with strict supervision would be the sequel. There is one aspect about her which is rather worrying, namely her propensity for irresponsible relationships with the opposite sex. These have been in abeyance for some time past but might revive if she were premanently at home and going to a day school but I think that this is a risk that one can justifiably take in her interests.

I must emphasise that it is the opinion of Dr Melvin of the Hammersmith Hospital, who has supervised her Diabetic condition, that from his point of view there is no objection to her going to an ordinary school. As I have said in my reports before there is only one thing that I believe is of importance in this respect and that is that somebody must make sure that she always injects her Insulin when she is in an unsettled mental state.

Before the question of an ordinary school is finally decided, I think a full report from her mother about her behaviour during the numerous week-ends she has been at home should be obtained and a visit from a social worker to her home where he could see not only Mrs Read but also her other children would be helpful. If the welfare officer is satisfied as the result of his investigations that home conditions are suitable and that she is not likely to disrupt the family I would suggest that an endeavour should be made to secure a vacancy for her in an ordinary school — not in her last one — and that subsequent measures should be instituted according to her progress. After surveying Susan's case over the whole time she has been here, in my opinion she has actually benefited greatly from the supervision and treatment she has received here.

Yours sincerely,

Donald Blair. M.A. MD D.P.M.
Consultant Psychiatrist

14th November, 1966

Rather sad today Pt says she was naughty at W/E making a noise with her hands. Pt says she did not associate with any boys at W/E stayed in all W/E. She has a mark on R. leg where her young sister jabbed her leg with a biro pen because she kept making her clapping noise. 'I am so unhappy as I am . . .'. Has written to her M. apologising for her behaviour, and making reference to the death of her father. Pt. says she is afraid she will never 'get out of here'. Reassured.

Charles Lovett.

Charles Lovett was shy and inoffensive. A bachelor with no family commitment other than an aged mother at home in Ireland, he devoted himself to his patients. He was gauche, he stammered, he blushed. He left an impression of adolescence that was difficult to reconcile with his near retirement.

Charles had not risen far in the medical hierarchy. He was

by temperament a second-in-command — a conservative man who was averse to risk and insecurity.

Female 19 was his responsibility.

> 19th January 1967
>
> Patient has made improvement while in Ward 19. W/S reports that she hasn't given the slightest trouble. She has accepted discipline; is most apologetic when reprimanded, says the offence will not be repeated — and it is not. Has had a few informal lessons with staff, and has shown self keen to learn. Ward Sister thinks she's fit to concentrate on school work, and might behave herself. Has not, however, taken her diet in the proper way recently — taking sweets from other patients, and eating at Art Therapy. Gives herself her Insulin injections.

The National Council for Civil Liberties had approached the Ministry of Health and received a reassuring reply.

> Ministry of Health,
> Alexander Fleming House,
> Elephant and Castle,
> London, S.E.1.
> 19th January, 1967

IN CONFIDENCE

Dear Mr Smythe,

You wrote to the Minister on 13th December about Susan Read who is a patient in St Bernard's Hospital.

From enquiries we have made of the Regional Hospital Board it seems that Susan has presented considerable difficulties to all who have tried to help her. Although she has been in a closed ward she has had a good deal of freedom including week-ends at home with her mother. However, it is clear that she has benefited considerably from the care she has received at St Bernard's Hospital. It is apparently arguable whether she needed formal psychotherapy as a form of medical treatment. The combination of firm, tactful and sympathetic handling she has received from St Bernard's may well have been in her best interests. Indeed, the

Consultant Psychiatrist at that hospital is now of the opinion that if Susan could live at home and attend a local school, this would be the best solution for her. He is anxious that Susan should start at a local school as soon as possible this term and I understand that the London Borough of Hillingdon are in close touch with the hospital with a view to deciding the most suitable arrangements for Susan's future.

Yours sincerely,

Private Secretary

MEDICAL OFFICER OF HEALTH

20th January 1967

Dear Dr Blair

Thank you for your letter of 18th January 1967, with the enclosures.

The day following the receipt of your letter Mrs Read rang Dr Bridger, Senior Medical Officer, stating that she had had a talk with Susan who was adamant that she wanted to return home and go to school and not go to any intermediate convalescent home. In the circumstances, therefore, Mrs Read agreed that Susan would return home this Friday, 20th, and begin school as arranged on 23rd January.

You will remember at our last meeting that Miss O'Donnell and Dr Bridger were to investigate the possibility of Susan beginning at Swakeleys Secondary Modern School for Girls and Mrs McNeill, the headteacher, had been approached and was willing for Susan to be given a trial of education at the school. I have also contacted Miss H. Carter, Health Visitor, who will support Mrs Read as much as possible and Dr Morgan, Psychiatrist at the Child Guidance Clinic, Uxbridge has given an initial interview appointment for Tuesday, 24th January, at 3.15 p.m. Mrs Read and Susan have both been invited to attend and Mrs Read has agreed. Dr Morgan has stated that she will see Susan at weekly intervals at least.

Susan will be given transport to school for the next few weeks and one of the teachers who is employed at Swakeleys School will accompany her on the journey.

I hope that these arrangements for Susan's future will bear fruit and that she can return to a more normal life in the weeks to come.

Thank you for your help over the past few months; it has been much appreciated.

MEDICAL OFFICER OF HEALTH

Correspondence was not Charles Lovett's strong point. He spent his time with the patients, and his desk was but a store for unattended papers. The first few days of his leave were always devoted to the backlog.

14th March 1967

Susan Read

· Admitted: 4.2.66   Discharged: 20.1.67

Behaviour disorder — Hypomaniac with underlying depression. Diabetes Mellitus

This girl was admitted as no other arrangements for her treatment could be made at the time.

She had been attending the Diabetic Clinic at Hammersmith Hospital for some time having been diagnosed in January 1965 as suffering from Diabetes Mellitus.

In March 1965 her father died suddenly from coronary thrombosis and following this she became very difficult to manage. At the same time her mother was depressed following her husband's death.

Susan was referred to Dr Hersov in the Psychological Medicine Department at Hammersmith Hospital.

For some time after admission here she was emotionally unstable, overactive and provoking towards other patients. She improved after transfer to a closed ward where there was firmer discipline and more control. As her condition improved she was given increasing freedom and allowed to go to Art Therapy etc.

Throughout her stay here she attended the Diabetic clinic at Hammersmith Hospital under the care of Dr Melvin.

Over a period of time she made considerable improvement and it was eventually thought best for her to return home and to attend her local school. Some points however will require attention.

1. Control of Diabetes. Susan injects her insulin herself.

The Diabetic Clinic at Hammersmith Hospital will maintain supervision and recommend any dosage change.

If patient should become disturbed or depressed extra supervision would be necessary to make sure that she was giving herself correct dosage.

There were several episodes in which Susan had a period of unconsciousness with or without a fit. Some of these occurring before her admission here and some during her stay here, all thought to have been due to hypoglycaemia occurring in the morning. Should any further attacks occur I am sure Dr Melvin would advise about any change in insulin dosage.

2. E.E.G tracings were done on two occasions. 'The E.E.Gs have been studied by Dr Allen Senior Neurological Registrar at Hammersmith Hospital who believes that the minor abnormalities present in both tracings can be attributed to the drug she was on and to drowsiness. She is confident that there is nothing significant in the E.E.G. of organic brain disease'. Dated 29th June 1966.

3. Educational. The girl's progress at school would of course depend upon her ability to attend regularly and to concentrate on her lessons. Intelligence tests done here suggested that she was of low average intelligence.

4. Medication. (Apart from insulin.)
     At time of departure:
          Haloperidol   3 mgs t.i.d.
          Disipal   100 mgs t.i.d.

This dosage will need review and it may be possible gradually to reduce the drugs.

Please get in touch with us should difficulties arise or should you require further information.

C.S. LOVETT MB. CH.B. DPM.

Comment

'As far as intelligence goes I think Susan is better than test results

171

show. It is impossible to put any value on the W.I.S.C. as Susan was playing up all the time.'

E.R. Psychology

20th March 1967.

Dear Dr MacGreevy,

As you know, I see Susan weekly for psychotherapy and her mother sees Mrs Glacklin, Psychiatric Social Worker.

Susan is very drowsy on her present tablets and though undoubtedly she does need sedation as she regularly gets into an over-active, excitable state, I am just wondering whether her sedation could be reduced gradually. I understand she is on Haloperidol 2 t.d.s. and Disipal 2 T.D.S. Perhaps they could be reduced to 1 t.d.s. and gradually discontinued over the next few months.

I am anxious to keep Susan out of hospital if we can, though St Bernard's would be prepared to re-admit her if this becomes inevitable. At present she has settled down reasonably well at Swakeley's School part time.

It seems to me that her silly over-active behaviour is a defence against depression and that the disturbance is basically a depressive one which came on following her father's death and her developing diabetes.

Margaret E. Morgan.
Medical Director.

Dr Morgan's fears were fulfilled — the Easter holidays were disastrous. The Health Visitor and social worker informed the Borough Medical Officer, and Dr Bridger in turn contacted Dr Lovett.

8.4.67

Dear Dr Lovett

Re: *Susan READ aged 13*

Re. our conversation over the phone this afternoon, I cannot contact Dr McGreavy the girl's G.P. as he is off duty. I have seen Mrs Read and Susan and would be grateful if you would see Susan as promised.

Susan's behaviour at home during the Easter Holidays has deteriorated according to the Health Visitor, Miss Carter, and the mother. She has threatened the small brother with a loaded hypodermic syringe of insulin. She informed the local police that she had been assaulted by a youth a fortnight ago. Last week she rang Scotland Yard and reported that her mother had struck her. She continually strikes her brother with fists, sticks and once threatened her mother with a carving knife (though it is doubtful if she would have carried out the threat).

Last evening she broke a window and it seemed to Mrs Read that she was unaware of her actions.

Most of her actions have appeared to be that of a 'naughty' child but now it seems to be of a more vicious nature.

I understand that Dr Morgan, Psychiatrist at Uxbridge Child Guidance Service has spoken to Dr Blair about Susan.

Thank you for your help.

J.W.E. Bridger,
Senior Medical Officer

Susan Read was taken back into Female 19. She was 13. The restrictions were softened. She went back to school each morning and she was granted ground parole.

In May Dr Lovett was replaced by Dr Walker. Pauline Walker was a spinster. It's an emotive word. She was no less married than bachelor Charles. Yet her soul had shrunk. A face set in a prim mould, a sober suit, a rigid scrawl.

PW/LS/F19   14th June, 1967.
CL/HH/303059
Dear Dr Lowy,

Re: Susan Read

Thank you for your letter of the 5th June, 1967. I have ascertained that Susan's diet in the ward is strictly adhered to (and this was the same diet on which, when she was continuously in hospital, the urine remained largely sugar free). I am afraid that now she goes to school and home for the weekends it is impossible to prevent her eating sweets and extra carbohydrates. She denies that she does this but she has, in fact, been seen with sweets by nursing staff. I saw her mother yesterday and she informed me that when Susan is at home at the weekends she has no control over her diet and that Susan eats cakes from the pantry, etc.

Yours sincerely,

P. Walker, MB, Ch.B. D.P.M.
Assistant Psychiatrist

Dr C. Lowy
Registrar to Professor Russell Fraser,
Hammersmith Hospital,
Du Cane Road,
Shepherds Bush, W.12.

2nd June, 1967

Appears happy, hypomanic. Was sexually provocative to a male patient yesterday.

Today announces that she loves her mother more than anyone in the world and is afraid to go home for fear she 'loses control' again.

Describes how she loses control when she sees a handsome boy. Feels she must follow them.
On Haloperidol   3 mgm   )
) t.d.s.
Disipal   2 tablets)

Pauline Walker

8th August 1967.
Behaved very badly over week-end. Mother found her impossible to control. Discovered exhibiting herself to boy-friend.

PW

26th Sept. 1967.
Has been associating with a male patient, at Industrial Therapy. Told her mother she had had sexual relations with him in the grounds of the hospital. (Patient is a borderline subnormal boy with a behaviour problem.) In view of danger of pregnancy she will have to be kept in ward at present.

PW

Dr Donald Blair was well liked and respected within the hospital, but now he was about to retire. His successor had not been appointed, and in the interim Dr Lovett would step into his place.

Dr Dobson, the Borough Medical Officer, made his contribution to the dilemma — two weeks at a holiday camp.

28th June 1967

Dear Dr Dobson
Susan READ born 31.10.53

Thank you very much for your letter about Susan. I have given the matter of her proceeding to the Holiday Camp full consideration and I have discussed it with her mother. I personally feel that she could go to this Camp on the following condition, that she should be told before she goes that if she misbehaves or upsets the other residents at The Camp, steps will be taken to return her to St Bernard's Hospital at once and only if it would be practical to return her to St Bernard's Hospital should the necessity arise, I think she should be allowed to go. Actually I believe that if she receives a firm warning it is unlikely that she will misbehave badly. There is one other point that I think is important, namely, that while she is there she should receive constant supervision by which I mean that she will not have the opportunity of wandering off with boys on her own. I understand from Mrs Read that there are a sufficient number of staff always to have the boys and girls under supervision even when they go in various parties to outings and I hope this is so. There is no doubt that Susan would benefit from a holiday at this Camp but I do not think that under any circumstances she should be allowed to exploit other people there and I think it would be to her advantage, that of the staff and the others who will be staying at the camp if the arrangements I have suggested above are fully implemented.

With reference to Susan's future, apart from anything to do with the Camp, matters are still extremely difficult. She is well-behaved at this hospital because she receives appropriate discipline and because she feels accepted and liked. Her mother tells me that at home she feels largely rejected and I fear this is so because she upsets her sisters and brother so much that they are not fond of her and must convey their feelings to her. Mother undoubtedly loves her and does everything she can to help but, again, at times cannot hide her feelings of distress and disapproval. I would suggest that for the time being the various procedures in being continue but during the coming holidays the question of her future will have to be carefully considered, the following points being very important:—

1. Will it be possible to attend her school on a full-time instead of a part-time basis.

2. Is it advisable for her to have another trial period staying at home all the time and if she does so will she have the opportunity of regular treatment from Dr Morgan's successor?

As you may know, I am retiring from the National Health Service on the 30th of this month but when my successor is appointed I shall make him fully aware of all aspects of this case. I shall still be doing private work and will be available for advice and help about Susan and if you want it please do not hesitate to get in touch with me. My telephone number is Welbeck 6178, and I shall be joining the staff at Bowden House Clinic at Harrow-on-the-Hill and the number there is Byron 1011.

DONALD BLAIR M.A. MD DPM.
CONSULTANT PSYCHIATRIST

Susan did not go on holiday. She also used offensive language in addressing the headmistress, and her attendance at school was terminated.

Dr Lovett tried again to seek a placement in an adolescent unit.

14th September 1967

Dear Dr Weihs

re: *Susan READ aged 13*

Thank you very much for seeing this girl. I understand that she will be accompanied by her mother, who will be able to give you a detailed history.

Susan suffers from moderately severe diabetes. She gives herself her insulin injections quite accurately and the diabetes is fairly well controlled. She occasionally has a hypoglycaemic episode. Last year she had several in the early mornings in which epileptiform fits occurred.

She has for some weeks been going regularly to a local girls' school on a part-time basis and appears to enjoy this.

When she first came to us she was very unruly, emotionally unstable and difficult in her behaviour, annoying other patients. She is now much less excitable and quite co-operative and affectionate but needs firm management. She 'tests out' people around her by using swear words but not in an aggressive way. She is playful and often gay and elated.

She is likely to behave in a provocative way towards boys and requires supervision on account of this. Menstruation has not yet commenced.

C.S. LOVETT MB. CH.B. DPM.
ASSISTANT PSYCHIATRIST

31st July 1967.

Dear Dr MacGreevy,

I have found that a Dr McClure, who at present is on the medical staff at the Bethlem Hospital, has been appointed to succeed Dr Blair at St Bernard's Hospital, but he has not yet taken over the post.

I have written to Dr McClure at the Bethlem Hospital giving him up-to-date details of Susan's case and I have asked him if he would consider Susan for an adolescent unit such as the one at the Bethlem Hospital, with the object of admission being on a long term therapeutic basis.

O.C. DOBSON.
MEDICAL OFFICER OF HEALTH

Dr McClure found another post. Dr Blair's position was now vacant and the team understaffed — two doctors could not properly care for over 800 patients.

Dr Birnie, the Medical Superintendent, advertised for a *locum tenens* to run the 'firm' for the three months it would take to appoint a consultant.

I answered that advertisement. Dr Birnie interviewed me. He found me too young, too brash, too radical. With obvious unhappiness he appointed me. I suspect I was the only applicant.

The hospital was a typical Victorian pile: school, barracks, prison — hospital cloned institutions. The original geometry was proportional and pleasing, but as the demand to house the lunatics of London inexorably rose, the buildings grew. Wings were attached, and wings grew wings; a third storey was added. The asylum changed from the open sun-filled wards of a country hospital to a darkened labyrinth. F19 was a dismal place. It was on the upper storey and 'land-locked' by bricks.

Though Ward 19 was described as a refractory ward, only a minority of the women there were violent or destructive. The majority were ageing and deteriorated. 'Mad' for many years, they stood in corners in anguished conversation with personal phantoms. They gibbered at mirrors, giggled at their own image, a reality they could control. They screamed, they wailed, they shouted.

Entry into the ward could be an unnerving experience, but by rapid adjustment of one's own perception of reality — a quick twist on the control knobs — one could quickly learn to smile blithely at the pictures on the screen.

Susan was skinny, with knobbly knees and a shy smile. Her face was a child's — charming, innocent and at odds with her fruity language. There was no psychiatric disorder detectable — no effectual imbalance, no illogicality of thought. There was much reported evidence of inadequate control — temper tantrums provoked by a mild admonition, rage in reaction to a petty frustration. Paradoxically, she tolerated the gross lunacy of her environment with equanimity. The essence of her 'madness' was that she persistently behaved in a manner that prompted authority to 'protect' her.

Susan needed to learn that there were wiser ways to express herself. We considered together the means by which such wisdom could be acquired. She committed herself to proving that 'sanity' was an option she was capable of choosing. I gave her the freedom of the hospital grounds to prove it.

In the meantime, the correspondence in pursuit of a healthier environment continued.

26th October 1967

Doctor in Charge
Adolescent Unit
Long Grove Hospital
Epsom
Surrey
Dear Doctor

re: *Susan Read aged 13*

This patient has been treated here from 4.2.66 to 20.1.67 and was readmitted on 8.4.67. She became disturbed and difficult to manage at home following her father's death in March 1965. Her mother subsequently became depressed for some time, a depression which continued after Susan's admission here.

Susan's diabetes is fairly well controlled — though she occasionally has a hyoglycaemic episode. Last year she had several in the early mornings in which epileptiform fits occurred.

She has been going regularly to a local school. Unfortunately a row with the headmistress led to their terminating her attendance.

I enclose a copy of a psychological report.

She is in a closed refractory ward with many chronically disturbed elderly patients. I am sure you will understand it is a most unsuitable environment for a fourteen year old.

Local schooling has proved to be unsatisfactory and the waiting lists at the Rudolph Steiner and other establishments are prolonged. The home situation remains unsatisfactory.

I would be grateful if you would consider her for transfer to your Adolescent Unit. She herself is enthusiastic about the idea and with the environment and kind of care you can provide I feel confident that her prognosis is good.

LESLIE MORRISH
CONSULTANT PSYCHIATRIST

31st October 1967

Dear Dr Morrish,
Susan READ. aged 13, d/b 31.10.53
9, Down Barnes Road, South Ruislip.

Thank you for your letter about the above patient but I am afraid she comes outside our area and in any case would not really be a suitable case for our Unit at the moment. I am sorry not to be more helpful.

Kind regards,

Yours sincerely,

Dr Peter Johnson.
Consultant of Adolescent Unit.

At least it was prompt.

The other prompt response came from the Medical Superintendent. News of Susan's licence was quickly channelled through. Dr Birnie came to Female 19 in person and cancelled ground parole.

Dr Bernard Baruch was appointed consultant. He was another dedicated man of integrity and intelligence. For years he had worked within the hospital, nominally assistant to the Medical Superintendent; in practice he had moulded a thera- peutic community out of a rag-bag of patients whose prognosis pointed to the long-stay wards. Because this was an internal promotion, there was no need for him to serve his three months' notice, so my temporary tenure ended. His move left the therapeutic community leaderless. I was available — so, in essence, Dr Baruch and I exchanged places.

It was not long before he too met Susan.

29th November 1967

Dear Dr Fowler,

I have myself interviewed Miss Read who was previously unknown to me. My opinion is that she is not suffering from psychosis nor from any neurotic illness. The diagnosis is character disorder, possibly aggravated by non-specific cerebral dysrhythmia.

She is a girl of normal intelligence, capable of warmth and affection and capable of responding to fair and firm handling.

Her character disorder becomes obvious when she is teased, provoked or treated unjustly. She then immediately reacts by a show of anger or outrageous behaviour of one sort or another, intended to shock and to repay injustice she imagines has been done to her.

The outbreak of the disorder coincided with the death of her father, and I feel that it is essential that she live and develop in a place where parental authority is exercised by both men and women. I therefore, agree with the plan to transfer her to a school for maladjusted children, with one important proviso, i.e. that it should be a school in which formal punishment of a retributive kind is not used, as such a regime would intensify Miss Read's present problem.

U.B.H. Baruch M.D. C.M. (Ont.) D.P.M.

15th December 1967.

Dear Dr Fowler,

I thought it might be helpful to you to supplement my letter of November 29th and let you know that on the initiative of the Medical Director of Uxbridge Child Guidance Clinic, Dr Urquhart, Mrs B. Miller, Psychotherapist, Mrs J. Clacking, Psychiatric Social Worker met Dr Walker and myself yesterday to discuss Miss Read's future. We unanimously agreed that it would be in Miss Read's interest to be transferred as soon as possible from this mental hospital and to be admitted to a school for maladjusted children which is known to handle children with firmness and sympathy rather than by harsh measures. We were further in agreement that it would help Miss Read to settle down in such a new place and it would be best for her future if psychotherapy were to continue without a break.

A school which would fulfil these conditions is, I understand, Pine End School for maladjusted girls, located at Reigate and administered by the Inner London Education Authority.

U.B.H. Baruch M.D. C.M. (Ont) D.P.M.

Ext. 65

UB/JMB/F.19
CL/CAA/303059

19th January, 1968

STRICTLY

CONFIDENTIAL

Dear Dr Lowy,

Miss Susan READ

You will recall that some weeks ago we had a conversation about this girl on the telephone and that at the time I said that if she were pregnant it would be most likely that I would be able to recommend termination of pregnancy on psychiatric grounds.

In my interview with her yesterday, Miss Read, who feels, I think, rightly that she is pregnant, was most enthusiastic about having a baby. She said that ever since her father died she had longed for a baby, which to her means having someone in the world who belongs to her and with whom she feels at one.

Since she has realised that she is pregnant she has completely stopped her sexual provocative behaviour and now feels apologetic about her past conduct. In retrospect she states that this behaviour was motivated by her desire to become pregnant.

I feel at the moment that termination of pregnancy would be experienced by Miss Read as an unforgivable act of robbery and therefore cannot recommend it. On the other hand she is sufficiently realistic to recognise that she would not be able to care fully for the baby for the present and would be prepared to have the baby fostered.

There may of course be overriding organic reasons why the pregnancy should be terminated and, if so, I would of course not oppose it.

Yours sincerely,

Dictated by: U.B.H. Baruch, M.D., C.M. (Ont.), D.P.M.
and signed in his   *Consultant Psychiatrist*
absence.
Dr C. Lowy
Registrar to Prof. Russell Fraser,
Hammersmith Hospital,
Du Cane Road, W.12.

Ref. GFJ/JT/303059   DU CANE ROAD

Tel. (01)-743 2030   SHEPHERDS BUSH, W.12

Ext. 65   2nd February, 1968

Dr U.B.H. Baruch, M.D., C.M. (Ont), D.P.M.
Consultant Psychiatrist
St Bernard's Hospital
Southall, Middx.

Dear Dr Baruch,
        Re: Miss Susan READ, aet 14
         9 Downbarnes Road, South Ruislip, Middx.

I am replying to your letter to Professor Russell Fraser of January 24th as he was away with pneumonia at the time that Mrs Read and Susan were at the diabetic clinic, but I myself was in touch with what was going on.

I am pleased to report first that the Latex pregnancy test done by Dr Lowy has proved to be negative. Mrs Read and Susan came back to the diabetic clinic on January 26th where I saw them again as Dr Lowy was on holiday. We found that there is a general slight excess of glycosuria throughout the day as shown by her own meticulous records, and so we have recommended an increase in morning N.P.H. to 30 units. We wrote this on her card.

The mother was most relieved to have heard both from yourself and on the 26th from us that Susan was not pregnant. Susan herself rather alarmed me by repeatedly expressing disappointment that she had not conceived. I gathered from Mrs Read that she had an appointment with yourself that afternoon to review the whole question of Susan's further management.

I have passed on the case notes and your letter to Professor Fraser, who has now returned to work, so as to keep him right in

the picture. We will continue, of course, to do everything we can to help in the management of this most tragic case.
Yours sincerely,

C.F. Joplin, Ph.D., M.R.C.P.
Lecturer in Clinical Endocrinology &
Consultant Physician

PW/HED/F19   29th February, 1968.
SCHOOLS/SSW/RF/PR.

Dear Sir,
                    re: Susan Read (31.10.53)
                    9 Down Barns Road, Ruislip.

Thank you for your letter of the 13th February. We would certainly be grateful if you could provide a visiting teacher for the above named and we will make arrangements about accommodation when you let us know the times the teacher will be available.
                              Yours faithfully,

                              P. Walker, M.B., Ch.B., D.P.M.
                              Assistant Psychiatrist

Chief Education Officer,
London Borough of Hillingdon,
Education Department,
Council Offices,
High Street,
Uxbridge,
Middx.

                    xxx   Dr C.S. Lovett
                           Dr U.B.H. Baruch
CSL/LS/F17   25th November, 1968.
                    Re: Miss Susan READ

Casualty Officer, Harrow Hospital, Dr Wood, telephoned 24th November to say that Susan had spent the night there — she had taken 40 junior aspirins — he thought in a gesture. She had been disturbed while home, complaining of being upset by patients in F18.

Interviewed Susan and her mother on 24th November — Susan appeared tense, twisting her face, and said she would not come back into hospital and requested three months leave. At the same time, she was cheerful in bouts and playful. After a discussion with mother granted one week's leave — for your advice regarding further management.

C.S. Lovett

6.2.69. Interview with the teacher of Miss Susan READ, F17.

Teacher says that for a long time Susan presented herself as a gentle saint incarcerated among wild and unpleasant women. However, she saw the other side of Susan recently when she flew into a rage and nearly attacked a coloured nurse. She has tried various projects, all of which interest Susan for some time but usually gets fed up. She has written some good essays and is fluent in expression. On the whole she is up to about 11 years old schooling level. The other day she was in a rebellious mood and swore at the teacher who decided to end the session on that occasion. At present, Susan wants to get a job and meet people. She says that she recently helped her sister, who is 19, in a filing office at B.E.A. where, according to Susan, she managed quite well. Is to have an interview with Mrs Bradshaw today at 2.30 p.m.

C.S. Lovett.

ST BERNARD'S HOSPITAL
SOUTHALL,
MIDDLESEX.
Tel. 01-574 5381-4
3rd March, 1969

Dear Dr Morrish,
   re. Miss Susan Read, (15)

   I would be grateful if you would consider having this girl in Connolly Ward. As you will see from the notes, she came to us at the age of 12 following the death of her father. She became acutely disturbed and has been a severe adolescent behaviour problem ever since. She is a diabetic and also has cerebral dysrhythmia.

   In the last three or four months there has been a marked improvement; we have been able to have her in an open ward. She attends regularly for lessons with a tutor appointed by the Education Authority and is hoping in April when she is 16 to begin a job. She is a very lively girl of average intelligence. I would see her stay in Connolly Ward as a further step away from institutional hospital life and I think the more regular contact with a doctor in a therapeutic community would now be of benefit to her. If you decide to take her, I would be grateful if you would ask for her transfer direct from Ward 17 Female, where she is now staying.

   I saw the mother last Friday, who tells me that Susan has been behaving well in recent months during her periods of leave.

   Thanks for your help,

                                        Yours sincerely,

                                        U.B.H. Baruch
                                        Consultant Psychiatrist

Dr L.W. Morrish,
Consultant Psychiatrist,
Connolly Ward.

LM/BK   31st December, 1969
Dear Dr MacGreevy,

                    Re: Susan READ

This young lady has made a fair go of things on the outside for
some time but it is essentially a question of staggering from crisis
to crisis. I am readmitting her primarily to take some of the heat
off, but with the aim of getting her to work from here.

                                        Yours sincerely,

                                        Leslie Morrish
                                        Consultant Psychiatrist.

Dr B.K.P. MacGreevy,
182 The Fairway,
South Ruislip,
Middlesex.

Tim Francis was an enthusiastic young house doctor, fresh
out of medical school and eager to learn. He was especially
drawn to the climate of Connolly, a little oasis where ideas
could survive less stunted than in the surrounding aridity.

Enthusiasm and experience are so often reciprocal.
Dr Francis's zeal was uncontrolled by cynicism, exaggerated
by his own emotional liability and inflamed by the adoration
of a provocative young lady.

Most men share the view that nothing is more therapeutic
for a neurotic female than a satisfying love affair — it is often
described with less delicacy — and Tim Francis was in love.
What could be more right than giving fully of himself to one
hungry for tenderness?

The General Medical Council didn't share this view of his
actions and Dr Francis ceased to work at the hospital.

Susan's notes contain a brief reference only.

'7.7.70   Alleged seduction by House Officer has led to much
         greater thoughtfulness of the implications of relation-
         ships — helping/hurting.'

Tim's act was self-destructive — a quasi-suicide — and
Susan's loving had abetted it.

23rd July 1970.

Dear Dr Stuart Horner,
  re Susan Read (31.10.53)

   Thank you for your letter concerning this young lady. She has indeed been a problem, stretching now over some years, and her behaviour remains erratic, irresponsible, calculated against the Society she feels has rejected her, and effectively as destructive to herself as to others. I think it fair to say, however, that she is genuinely making conscious efforts to control this behaviour and responds well to new opportunities which she feels give her a fresh start free from the 'prejudices' of the adult world. I would not see her as in any way dangerous to young children, with whom she is likely to relate well and therefore would have no hesitation in recommending her for such a post. As far as she is concerned, residential employment, i.e. away from home and hospital, would be most beneficial. The difficulties I would foresee would be with her peers and authority and I think there should be no doubt to her prospective employers that there will be a need to deal with her as a patient as much as as an employee.

                                   Yours sincerely,

                                   Leslie Morrish
                                   Consultant Psychiatrist.

J. Stuart Horner, Esq., M.B., Ch.B., D.P.M., D.I.H.,
Director of Health & Welfare Services,
Health & Welfare Department,
Council Offices,
High St.,
Uxbridge.

TSR/MAL

DISCHARGE SUMMARY REPORT

MOUNT VERNON HOSPITAL, NORTHWOOD, MIDDLESEX.
Northwood 26111

Under the care of:— V. EDMUNDS, M.D., F.R.C.P.

NAME: Susan READ	AGE: 16	HOSPITAL No.: 70/4567
ADDRESS: 9 Down Barns Road,	OCCUPATION:	DATE OF BIRTH:
South Ruislip,	DOCTOR'S NAME:	ADMITTED: 17.9.70.
Middlesex.	Dr MacGreevy	
TEL. NO.		
M.S.W.D.	ADDRESS: The Fairway	DISCHARGED: transferred to
SEX:	South Ruislip	St Bernard's
	Middlesex.	18.9.70

DIAGNOSIS: SUMMARY also sent to:
OVERDOSE:

History: This girl was admitted on 17th September having taken an over-
                    dose.

H.P.C   She had taken an overdose of Epanutin and Ospalot probably 18
                    tablets. She is a diabetic on Insulin on 12 units of Soluble and 32
                    units of Soluble b.d. She was put on Epanutin and Ospalot at
                    St Bernard's.

On Examination: She was conscious but confused. She repeated the same answers
                    over and over again.

C.V.S.   Pulse rate was 84 per minute regular. B.P. 120/60. Heart sounds
                    were normal. There was a short systolic murmer to the left of the
                    sternum.

R.S.   Trachea was central. Breath sounds vesicular. No adventitious
                    sounds heard.

A.S.   N.A.D.

C.N.S.   Pupils were equal reacting to light. Reflexes were brisk, there was
                    no neck stiffness.

                    Blood sugar was 300 mg%. She was given 16 units of Insulin stat
                    and was put on four hourly sliding scale. She was noisy and
                    uncontrollable that night and was trying to run away. She was
                    seen by the Mental Welfare Officer in the morning and was
                    transferred to St Bernard's.

                                        T.S. RAVIKANT, Registrar to,
                                        V. EDMUNDS, M.D., F.R.C.P.

103A High Street
Ruislip
Middlesex
1 October 1970

Dr Morrish
Connolly Ward
St Bernard's Hospital
Southall

Dear Dr Morrish,
I am the sister of your patient Susan Read, and I understand from her that you think it would be a good idea for Susan to live with me. Before this matter gets out of hand, I would like to point out certain difficulties which must be taken into consideration.
1   Susan needs a special diet, which would be very expensive
2   Susan has difficulty in keeping a job
3   I share a flat with 2 other girls and Susan doesn't get on with them
4   Susan has suicidal tendencies
Apart from these points, I earn only enough to keep myself and can't possibly stretch my finances to include an extra expense. I have to work full-time and would not be able to take time off whenever Susan needed company or nursing. Also I am not yet 21 and am unqualified to take on such a heavy responsibility.

I have been wondering if it would be possible to get Susan into the Rudolph Steiner School, Aberdeen. There was a place for her at this school about 2 years ago, but Susan decided to go out to work instead. However, she has said recently during discussion that she would not mind going back to school. I would be pleased, therefore, if you could make some enquiries in this direction.

Yours sincerely,

Pamela Read

LM/MK   6th October, 1970.

The Secretary
Rudolph Steiner House,
35 Park Road,
LONDON, N.W.1

Dear Sir,

re Susan READ,
9 Down Barnes Road,
South Ruislip.

This young lady I understand is still on your waiting list. I do not seem to have all the correspondence but I have been informed that she was offered a place two years ago. I am writing now to find if such placement is still available to her. She is, in my view, very much in need of the kind of help that you can offer, but has now attained the age of sixteen. If you require information concerning the history of the last few years, I will be happy to oblige.

Yours sincerely,

Leslie Morrish,
Consultant Psychiatrist.

ANTHROPOSOPHICAL SOCIETY
IN GREAT BRITAIN

TELEPHONE   RUDOLPH STEINER HOUSE
723 4400   35 PARK ROAD
                                         LONDON, N.W.1.

Mr Leslie Morrish
St Bernard's Hospital
Southall
Middlesex   12 October 1970

Dear Sir,
Thank you for your letter of 6 October, but I think there must be some misunderstanding. We have no facilities here for placing patients, nor indeed the competence to do so. We can only send

to enquirers our booklet Practical Activities listing all our homes and schools in this country, pointing out that each is autonomous and further enquiries should be made direct to the centre concerned. Although I cannot trace any correspondence on Susan Read I imagine this would have been the procedure in her case, and that the waiting list to which you refer is at one or other of the schools in the booklet. But no doubt your files will contain some correspondence relevant to this.

I am sorry not to be more helpful. If you haven't a copy of Practical Activities I would be happy to send one. It costs 2s6d and a postal order for this is always acceptable.

Yours faithfully,

M. Alexandra (Mrs.)
Organising Secretary

LM/MK.   25th January, 1971.

Dear Dr MacGreevy,
                          Susan READ,
                          9 Down Barnes Road,
                          SOUTH RUISLIP.
              Admitted: 15.1.71.   Discharged: 18.1.71.

   This young lady was admitted on a seventy-two hour order
following an epileptic attack, almost certainly due to hypoglycaemia, and followed by post-epileptic automatism. There
would appear to be nothing here to indicate placement on
Section. One must assume that her arrival here was largely at the
instigation of her poor harassed mum who frequently feels that
she can take no more and wishes us to share the burden from
time to time! On examination it was apparent that Susan was as
well as she has been for the last couple of years and I felt that
further detention would not be legal.

                                        Yours sincerely,

                                        Leslie Morrish,
                                        Consultant Psychiatrist.

Dr B. MacGreevy,
182, The Fairway,
SOUTH RUISLIP.

The official correspondence petered out as the tie between
Susan and hospital was steadily loosened.
   Susan learned the rules of the game and earned her freedom.
The hospital was no longer her home, the staff no more *in
loco parentis.* She was officially erased from the register of
patients.
   It has taken longer for the hospital to be erased from
Susan's record.